MW01702779

Words About Bounce Back and Win

"What a great way to show how persistence pays off! Lets hope it becomes required reading in colleges everywhere."

TOM CORMACK, VICE PRESIDENT,
Personnel Systems Corp.

"This book capsules the outlook that is vital for anyone who wants to move beyond where they are."

KEVIN SCHMIDT, MANAGING PARTNER,
Envisionworks, Inc.

"Wow! My lasting impression after reading Bounce Back and Win *was that it would be the best possible gift for everyone who changes jobs—whether they are fired, downsized or leave voluntarily."*

JAMES E. PEHTA, FOUNDER, LPC, Inc.
currently—Pitney Bowes Software Systems

Other Books by Roger Fritz

What Managers Need to Know

Productivity and Results

Performance Based Management

Rate Yourself as a Manager

You're in Charge: A Guide for Business and Personal Success

The Inside Advantage

Nobody Gets Rich Working for Somebody Else

Personal Performance Contracts

If They Can—You Can! Lessons from America's New Breed of Successful Entrepreneurs

Rate Your Executive Potential

Management Ideas That Work

How to Export: Everything You Need to Know to Get Started

Ready, Aim, HIRE! (Co-author)

The Entrepreneurial Family: How to Sustain the Vision and Value in Your Family Business

Think Like a Manager

Sleep Disorders: America's Hidden Nightmare

Sales Manager's High Performance Guide: The Only Reference You Need to Build a Powerful Sales Force

A Team of Eagles

How to Manage Your Boss

The Small Business Troubleshooter

Wars of Succession

America Behind Bars: Bold New Ways to Fit Punishment With Crime

One Step Ahead, The Unused Keys to Success

On CD-ROM

The Personal Business Coach

Beyond Commitment: The Skills All Leaders Need

BOUNCE BACK AND WIN

ROGER FRITZ

Copyright © 1999 Roger Fritz

This edition published by
Raffles, an imprint of
SNP Editions Pte Ltd
162 Bukit Merah Central
#06-3545
Singapore 150162
Fax: (65) 276 6970
Website: http://www.snp.com.sg

First published in 1999 by Inside Advantage Press (USA)

All rights reserved. No part of this publication
may be reproduced, stored in a retrieval system,
or transmitted in any form or by any means,
electronic, mechanical, photocopying, recording
or otherwise, without prior permission of
the publishers.

Project Editor – Wong Wan Ling
Cover design by Deon Chee Leehua

ISBN 981-4032-71-9

Printed by SNP Offset (M) Sdn Bhd

For Steve King
Whose persistence and resilience are exceeded
only by his humility and generosity

Contents

Introduction

Who Needs This Book?

If you have recently suffered a career setback, if you are disappointing yourself, if you feel you're not measuring up to the expectations of others, or if you are discouraged by what looks like an unending string of bad luck, this book is for you.

That's because the key to success in life is not brilliance, or agility, or competence, or even experience. It's recovery—the ability to bounce back from adversity.

Those who bounce back tend to win, because they persist and survive while others give up and quit. Procrastinators lose any advantage they may have had. Dropouts aren't even in the competition. Excuse-makers are their own worst enemy.

Abe Lincoln said it best: "All things come to those who wait—but they get only what's left over by those who hustle."

Very few of God's children are *always* self-motivated. Most of us need some help to be our best. That's what this book is all about. It contains ideas that will challenge and provoke you. It asks questions you may find difficult to answer. It is intended to help you master the techniques of *resilience* and *persistence*, two qualities that are essential for bouncing back and overcoming adversity.

We will explore *resilience* as the key to immediate success and *persistence* as the only route to a continuing flow of rewards and personal satisfaction. Specifically, you will learn:

- How to benefit from temporary setbacks.
- Positive ways to overcome adversity.
- The advantages of persistence.
- Why confidence grows with achievement.
- How to build on strengths and minimize weaknesses.
- How to anticipate change as a competitive weapon.

Bad times introduce you to yourself.

You will be asked to work through nine steps and answer nine critical questions. Each requires the most honest and objective answer you can give. The hard, cold reality is that unless and until they are answered, progress is doubtful and success impossible. They are:

- How well do you know yourself?
- Are you ready for change?
- Are you convincing?
- Can you control yourself?
- Is time on your side?
- Are you confident?
- Who needs you?
- Who will help you?
- Will you use everything you have?

It is possible to bounce back—and find yourself even better off than you were before. I know firsthand about adversity. When I was fifteen, I had polio. For many months I was so preoccupied with feeling sorry for myself that I became my own worst enemy. My attitude turned around when I decided to take my partial paralysis as a challenge to overcome. I realized that if good things were going to happen again, I would have to make them happen myself. Fortunately, my parents never said, "Don't worry, we'll take care of you." Looking back on it, I honestly think that having polio at that young age is one of the better things that happened to me.

To me, the question is how long will you allow yourself to engage in regret or self-pity? My recommendation is five seconds. Time's up! Prepare now to *Bounce Back and Win!*

—Roger Fritz

Successful people don't try to change the wind,
they reset their sails.

Step 1

How Well Do You Know Yourself?

Everything starts with you. Unless and until you understand yourself, you will be handicapped in understanding a job, an employer, friends and relatives, or any kind of relationship.

Self-knowledge is a blend of knowing what you value—that is, what you are willing to devote time, effort, and energy to—and having a keen grasp of your personal strengths and weaknesses. Unless you are objective about your assets and liabilities, the liabilities (your weaknesses) will prevail. You will never get close to achieving your potential when you let that happen.

First Law of Survival: Respect Yourself

Self-knowledge can also sustain you through difficult times. An understanding of your values is essential to developing the persistence that will see you through to your goals no matter what. Use this chapter to begin to examine your strengths and weaknesses and lay the foundation of purpose and persistence on which you can build your recovery.

YOU THINK *YOU'VE* FAILED?

How would you feel if you had suffered the defeats of this man, whose age at the time of each setback appears in the column on the right?

	Age
Failed in business	22
Ran for legislature—defeated	23
Again failed in business	24
Elected to legislature	25
Sweetheart died	26
Had a nervous breakdown	27
Defeated for Speaker	29
Defeated for Elector	31
Defeated for Congress	34
Elected to Congress	37
Defeated for Congress	39
Defeated for Senate	46
Defeated for Vice President	47
Defeated for Senate	49
Elected President of the United States	51

That's the record of Abraham Lincoln, whose leadership earned a lasting place in our country's history.

How did Lincoln overcome so many defeats and personal setbacks to achieve his goal of becoming president? The answer is *purpose and persistence.*

THE POWER OF PURPOSE

Abraham Lincoln was not only persistent, he had a strong sense of purpose. The power of purpose is tremendous. Without purpose, little is accomplished. With it, practically anything is possible.

Because of his burning purpose, Abraham Lincoln was able to forge ahead even when no one else believed in him. Ultimately, this enabled him to turn around his record of defeat. During the Civil War, his determination to keep the Union together helped him remain optimistic despite defeat after defeat in early battles.

Unfortunately, purpose requires a type of dedication that most people seem unwilling to give. Most of us wilt and withdraw when we are criticized or when someone questions our purpose.

Consider, for example, J. P. Morgan's letter to Alexander Graham Bell in 1875, which stated, "Mr. Bell, after careful consideration of your invention, while it is a very interesting novelty, we have come to the conclusion that it has no commercial possibilities." Or recall the British Parliament's report to Thomas A. Edison in 1878 concerning his notion of the light bulb: "Good enough for our transatlantic friends, but unworthy of the attention of practical or scientific men." Or jump to 1945, when Admiral Leahy reported to President Harry Truman, "the [atom] bomb will never go off, and I speak as an expert in explosives."

Purpose is important in any human endeavor. It is the beacon that lights our way in times of self-doubt, criticism, or temporary defeat. Purpose shows the way, while persistence keeps you going!

DEFINING YOUR PURPOSE

If it's true that time heals all wounds, then it's possible that your recovery *could* happen without your taking responsibility for it, but you'll get better results if you know your purpose and can direct yourself toward it.

Even when we have defined our purpose, however, we can become our own worst enemy in attaining it. To bring ourselves into a positive frame of mind, we must ask some important questions:

- Where am I headed?
- Am I devoting my time to what is most important to me?

- How would I like to spend the next five years?

Answering these questions is an essential part of getting to know yourself, which is the first step in bouncing back.

Milton Glaser asked his students at New York's School of Visual Arts to "design a perfect day for yourself five years from now." There are all kinds of similar exercises—such as writing your own obituary—that can help you determine your purpose. When taken seriously, such exercises can help to release people who are trapped not so much by circumstances as by lack of imagination.

Without imagination, there can be no alternatives and no motivation. The better you understand your hopes, dreams, and purpose, the faster you will be able to get back on track.

THE POWER OF PERSISTENCE

Most people, at some point in their lives, reach a career "dead spot." Promotions no longer come as frequently as they once did. Salary increases come less often and are smaller than they would like them to be. For some people, the dead spot is more dramatic, taking the form of an unexpected layoff or the loss of an important customer or client.

> **When prosperity comes,**
> **do not use all of it.** —Confucius

The major cause for the dead spot is complacency. People tend to fall into certain routines—some good, some bad—failing to change as conditions change. They stop analyzing and modifying their own performance standards to remain personally competitive, eventually losing their edge.

By contrast, Abraham Lincoln undoubtedly took stock of what

wasn't working and tried something new. He persisted until he found a strategy that worked.

As an avid golfer, I sometimes like to compare the requirements of successful people to those of top professional golfers. Gary Player is a great example. His accomplishments are legendary. He has not only won more tournaments worldwide than any other golfer, he is also a very successful course designer, rancher, and businessman.

I have spent some time with Player and discovered that he is a champion not because his golf balls or clubs are any different from yours or mine, but because he has learned to concentrate on the *basics* of the game, to *practice* those basics regularly, and to be *consistent* whenever he puts them to use. He is no more "gifted" than you or I. His shot may hook or slice off the tee. He may wind up in a sand trap. He may miss a two-foot putt. But he is successful because he has made it a habit to *analyze* mistakes, *determine* what caused them, and then *practice* diligently to see that he doesn't repeat them.

To escape a career dead spot or bounce back from a professional setback, you need to approach your work in exactly the same way. You must return to the basics of your craft, practice those principles consistently on the job, and learn from your mistakes. When problems occur, you need to discover what caused them and then practice the basics diligently to see that the same kind of mistake does not recur.

Whenever you encounter a setback or believe you may have reached a dead spot, it is time for serious self-evaluation. Too often we begin to look for a scapegoat—a condition, an individual, or a circumstance of some sort to which we can transfer the blame. This excuse-making never corrects the problem or prevents it from happening again.

When you transfer blame, you are making your inadequacies

obvious by revealing that you do not have the situation under control. Instead, you should ask these questions:

- Have I been shooting for an unrealistic goal?
- Was my goal the *right* goal?
- Did I understand the requirements for completion?
- Did I misinterpret anything?
- Have I used time and resources wisely?
- Do others have appropriate incentives to help me?

Only by taking the time to analyze your own role can you take positive, immediate action to correct inadequacies. Only then can you be assured that you are keeping your skills finely tuned, which is the best possible protection against reaching a dead end in your career.

Be a realist, not a perfectionist. You are bound to make mistakes. It is as unreasonable to expect every project to be an unqualified success as it is for Gary Player to expect to win every golf tournament. The objective is to come in near the top—to maintain a consistently high level of performance.

This continuous self-analysis is far better than adjusting to a crisis.

WHY SELF-KNOWLEDGE COMES FIRST

With persistence and purpose, you can overcome almost anything. But first you must have a good understanding of what make you tick.

Too much time is wasted, too many errors are made, and too many problems are created by those who don't really know who they are. Usually, it's because they either avoid the issue, procrastinate, or find a convenient alibi for their actions. If they knew they had a problem in being honest and objective about themselves, they could begin to overcome it.

How Well Do You Know Yourself?

How well do you understand yourself?

To find out, rate yourself on a scale of 0 to10 on each of the items listed below. Giving yourself a 0 would mean that you are absolutely lacking the quality described; 5 means average; and 10 means you have more of this quality than anyone you've ever known.

		Score
1.	I am well qualified for my job and the skills it involves.	______
2.	I am very persuasive and usually get others to agree with me.	______
3.	I get along well with others.	______
4.	I am honest, not only with myself, but with others.	______
5.	I have great powers of concentration; very little distracts me.	______
6.	I very quickly learn anything I put my mind to.	______
7.	I am a natural leader, always in the center of groups making things happen.	______
8.	My health and stamina are excellent; I never feel too tired to do what I have to do.	______
9.	I am self-disciplined and do what is required.	______
10.	I am decisive, quick and sure in my choices.	______
11.	I am well organized.	______
12.	I have a great deal of courage and am ready to forge ahead without letting fear hold me back.	______
13.	I am creative, have new ideas, and am ready to hear the ideas of others.	______
14.	I am able to catch on quickly and figure out situations rapidly.	______
15.	I have good judgment and often get hunches that I can follow to successful conclusions.	______
16.	Other people recognize my leadership and are willing to follow.	______
17.	I work well in a team situation and let others participate in making decisions.	______
18.	I think I have great potential for improving my abilities and my personality.	______
19.	I am satisfied with my present goals at work and feel comfortable and optimistic about achieving them.	______
20.	I have great energy, drive, and motivation to achieve my personal goals, and I feel confident that I am using my energy wisely in meeting them.	______

Don't bother adding up a score. Scores don't matter. The point is that every item above on which you have *honestly* rated yourself *below a 5* is an area of weakness. Now that you are aware of the problem, you can make a conscientious and sustained effort to improve.

Self-Knowledge and Effectiveness

To succeed, you must be deeply committed to self-development, lifelong learning, and staying on top of emerging trends. To stay the same is to fall behind. Studies show that the most effective people exhibit the following traits:

1. **They are effective in dealing with people.** They keep the organization working purposefully and harmoniously. They approach problems not only in an orderly way, but with a feel for humanity. They are thoughtful, tactful, and careful. As they strive for improved performance, they consistently maintain the respect (and usually the goodwill) of those around them.
2. **They are self-motivated.** They manage themselves efficiently and constantly develop their supervisory capabilities. They eagerly seek out new ideas and new techniques, then implement them.
3. **They understand the need for results.** Efficient people do things right. Effective people do the right things the right way. Leaders rely on information and facts to help stabilize performance and plan more accurately.
4. **They identify key result areas** and measures of progress. Split-second decision-making isn't a requirement. The effective person thoroughly thinks through what must be done, then takes the necessary action.

To be wise, think and study.
To be successful, execute.

Those who overlook these tasks often fall short of their early promise. Over the past forty years, Sears, Roebuck & Co. has conducted dozens of studies to determine the characteristics that inhibit success in an organization. They discovered the following common reasons for failure and ways to combat them.

Myopia. Some executives are effective at short-range planning and day-to-day supervision, but they are unable to foresee trouble spots or shape long-term strategies.
Ask Yourself:

- Do I consider organizational objectives in setting my personal goals?
- When giving directions, do I outline what results I expect?
- Do I maintain close contact with people whose broader perspective could benefit me?

Low Sociability. Inability to get along with a variety of people can stifle career progress.
Ask Yourself:

- Am I easy to talk to, or do I interrupt or dominate?
- How well do I put people at ease when first meeting them?
- Do I present ideas interestingly, or do people tend to glaze over or get impatient when I speak?

Overaggressiveness. This defect can keep us locked into a holding pattern. A certain amount of aggressiveness is necessary, but not when it is out of control.

Ask yourself:

- Do I tend to put people on the defensive?
- Must I always have control?
- Do I put people down?
- Am I reluctant to share the spotlight?

Undisciplined Judgment. Some people are smart but fail to put their intelligence to practical use or do not apply it consistently. Ask yourself:

- Do I tend to make decisions too quickly?
- Do I sometimes let my emotions dictate when impartiality is needed?
- Do I tend to be disorganized?

Whatever the reason for not going the distance, honesty is the vehicle that will deliver the answers you need. Looking at yourself critically can be painful, but once you discover the reasons for your behavior, you can work at correcting it and go on to realize personal goals.

ARE YOU "AVERAGE"?

Over the past half-century, too many Americans have "neutered" themselves mentally.

It is no longer fashionable to be exceptional, outstanding, unusual, or unique. Today, "average" is the term that many people believe to be "politically correct."

But, is that good?

Consider the definition of "average." If you don't have one of your own, use mine: If something is average, it is simply the best of the worst, or the worst of the best.

The man on the street today is all too often willing to settle for mediocrity. Mediocrity in the education he receives, mediocrity in the products he buys, mediocrity in the public officials he elects, mediocrity in all facets of his workaday existence.

Average . . . mediocre . . . the words are practically synonymous. The best of the worst or the worst of the best.

How did this situation arise?

Education without common sense is hollow.

1. We have failed to focus on performance.

We frequently fail to set a good example for the people around us, whether they are our children, other members of the family, or our business associates.

Of course, it is difficult for people to know what is expected of them unless they are properly supervised. Performance standards must be established before they can be followed.

Beyond some cursory job descriptions, few employers produce meaningful performance standards against which their employees can gauge the quantity and quality of their work.

Too often, when people are hired, it is more because of whom they know, how they look, or where they went to school than for their job-related qualifications.

When the performance of such employees later proves to be substandard, those who were responsible for hiring them may be too embarrassed to admit to having made a mistake to do anything about correcting the situation.

It may be faster and easier to handle a particular job yourself than to teach somebody else to do it, but if you do that you're holding yourself back, as well as the other person who might benefit from the experience.

True achievers often make waves. They accomplish more because they find new ways to do things, they experiment, they push the limits. They also tend to break the rules, incur the envy of their associates, and on occasion show up their superiors.

Employers often prefer to engage people who simply maintain the status quo, but in so doing, they bind themselves to the past and foreclose the opportunity to lead the way into the future.

2. We have allowed ourselves to settle for substandard results. We too often take the course of least resistance. As long as a child brings home a "C" on his report card, many parents will accept that instead of pressing for an "A" or "B," even though they know that the child is capable of doing better work. Why? Because it is less stressful, it avoids arguments, it is easier than having to monitor the child more closely, and "After all, it's a passing grade, isn't it?"

Employers often do nothing about it when their employees fail to perform as well as they should because it is "too difficult" to release an employee and then hire and train a replacement—and besides, "They may sue us and win!"

This is particularly true if the employee belongs to a union, holds a civil service position, or is tenured.

When a store clerk is out of a given product, often he or she can convince customers that some other, unknown brand is just as good.

American automobile manufacturers install radios that accept magnetic tapes and compact disks in their cars but no longer equip them with decent spare tires.

On occasion, they have sacrificed their customers' comfort and safety to cut costs and increase profits. They may install federally mandated seat belts for passenger safety, for example, and then put their gas tanks someplace where they will be prone to rupturing, fire, and explosion if the vehicle is involved in a collision.

Who is to blame for this state of affairs?

We all are, because we do not *insist* on the very highest levels of quality and performance, whether we are purchasing a product, patronizing a business, supervising an employee, or educating one of our children.

As I grow older, I pay less attention to what men say. I just watch what they do.—*Andrew Carnegie*

3. We tend to over-manage our most competent people. For a number of reasons, people often seem to be hesitant to turn top performers loose—to give them free rein. When we restrict such individuals, of course, we prevent them from fulfilling their potential.

We are equally hesitant to accept any suggestions that involve change and innovation.

If we try something different and it fails, we can be severely criticized. Sticking with the tried and true provides a comfortable safety net. There's a great deal of comfort in being able to say, "We've always done it that way."

Too often, knowingly or unknowingly, we penalize employees for their outstanding performance.

But avoiding failure is not the same as success. To be sure, if you spend your life trying to avoid failure you may be safer, but you will never experience the unique joy and satisfaction of creating more than God gave you.

The reward for doing good work is often more work, but if that extra work is not accompanied by additional compensation, it is a penalty, not a reward.

Too many people feel that they cannot promote someone under their supervision without jeopardizing their own chances for advancement. Just the opposite is true.

A wise leader knows that it is as important to have friends of equal or higher rank when it comes to advancement as it is to have a loyal and dedicated following. Nothing is more likely to produce a loyal and dedicated staff than their knowledge that the boss will not stand in the way of their advancement.

4. We focus on other people's weaknesses and fail to capitalize on their strengths.

A person's weaknesses may be short-lived. They may be due to nothing more than inadequate experience or training.

A person's strengths, however, can be prolonged, built upon, and expanded. Concentrate on the characteristics that can be most valuable to you: the person's strengths, not his or her weaknesses.

A person's weaknesses can often be transformed into something useful and positive.

Dwelling on the fact that a weakness can lead to failure may become a self-fulfilling prophecy.

Before criticizing a person's shortcomings, decide how significant the shortcomings are to begin with.

Unless they are in an area that's absolutely critical to the individual's ability to their work, they're not worth dwelling on.

5. We don't take the time to analyze our strengths and learn how to capitalize on them at work.

Get to know yourself well by identifying and then learning to overcome any weaknesses. Once the weaknesses are gone, all that is left are your strengths.

Don't spend a great deal of time searching for your weaknesses; other people will quickly point them out to you. Instead, make every effort to define what your strong points are and determine how you can use them to your best advantage.

Your strengths are of no value to you unless and until you put them to work. Strengths not put into service will shrink. Furthermore, failing to make use of the strengths you have will only cause you to work longer and harder than necessary.

6. We reward the wrong things, like busyness and seniority.

Many people become quite expert at giving the impression of being busy. They always walk quickly and carry a handful of papers, even if they're only headed for the rest room.

Some people actually have to work harder than their peers to accomplish the same amount of work. They should not be penalized for that, but neither should they be rewarded for it.

Seniority is not a substitute for good work. It can even be harmful if it helps to perpetuate outmoded methods, stifles progress, or hampers badly needed change.

A great deal of time and effort is spent on finding and attempting to refine latent talent. I believe you will be much better off utilizing talent that is already developed.

7. We try to build organizations around people who are dependent on us.

Too often, we shy away from hiring extremely competent people because we are afraid that we won't be able to hang onto them.

Perhaps our fears will be realized. But it's better to get five years of work out of a top performer than ten years out of a mediocre one.

Don't be so paranoid about losing a top performer that you literally create a self-fulfilling prophecy.

The fear that a good person might leave the company has actually been known to drive away the very person you sought to keep. Rather than worry about losing them, try to see what you will have to do to retain them.

If your competitors don't want your people, there must be a reason.

Dependency is a weakness, not a strength. It should be treated cautiously, not rewarded.

8. We allow incompetent people to hide behind a title and abuse their office.

In many instances, the current practice of downsizing a business amounts to nothing more than reducing a staff that has been allowed to grow top-heavy, unwieldy, and inefficient.

Executives who no longer are capable of pulling their own weight should either be given other responsibilities or moved out of the firm. They set a poor example for other employees and, in some cases, are an actual turnoff to customers.

What's the Cure?

Whenever you work with others, follow these suggestions to confront the effects of mediocrity head on:

1. Solicit the participation of others when you plan. The more ideas and fresh points of view you can draw upon, the more satisfactory and progressive the outcome is likely to be.
2. Negotiate clear, objective performance contracts. In other words, be specific in letting people know what you want and what you are willing to do in return.
3. Talk frequently with those who do the work. Don't depend on memos, and don't wait for the "perfect" time to criticize or to praise.
4. Listen to opinions, but when it is time to make a decision rely on facts and objective evidence.
5. Reward those who contribute most to progress, not those who do everything they can to resist it.
6. Criticize in private, but praise in public.
7. Select those who will be accountable for their actions. Avoid those who want you to decide.

8. Always determine *who* is to do *what* by *when*.

The cure for headlong plunge into mediocrity is not to be found in promises of politicians, or in credentials, or even in our institutions of education and government. It will be found only in the resolve of individuals to set and meet their own higher standards.

> **I have my faults, but being wrong ain't one of them.**—*Jimmy Hoffa*

SO YOU FAILED

You are not unique. Everyone encounters failure at some time in their lives. The most important thing you can do with failure is learn how to cope with it.

- **Realize that you are not perfect, nor is anyone else.** We all are subject to mistakes—that is, failure. The surest way to avoid failure is to do nothing, but you never will get anywhere doing nothing. Therefore, give yourself permission to fail once in a while.
- **Determine whether it is failure that disturbs you or the rejection that's often associated with failure.** If it's the latter, learn to cope with rejection, and failure no longer will haunt you.
- **Decide which is more important, avoiding failure or doing something worthwhile.** If you're constantly striving to do something worthwhile, you'll have no time to worry about an occasional failure.
- **Don't be intimidated by failure.** Failure is one of the laws of life. Learn to be somewhat fatalistic about it. Everyone who has ever bought a lottery ticket knows that there's very

little likelihood of winning. Everyone who has ever played a card game—or a board game like Monopoly, or Clue—knows that there must be a loser as well as a winner; and although we all play to win, the odds usually are at least 50-50 that we will lose. It is the same in business. You win some and you lose some. The secret is this: you should try to win more often than you lose, and try never to lose in critical situations.

- **Be able to separate personal failures from team failures.** If the quarterback on a football team gets sacked, he's not a failure. He failed to get the play away because someone else failed to provide a block. The blocker isn't a failure, either. Nine out of ten times, he does his job well. A single miscue does not make him a failure. Remember, his opponent was trying just as hard as he was to be successful.
- **Don't blame others as a means of making failure more personally tolerable.** You can't really kid yourself. All you can do is add a layer of guilt to your discomfort. Analyze the failure to see what caused it, not who. Then take steps to see that it does not happen again.
- **Accept failure as a part of the learning process.** As children, we learn to walk by standing, falling, rising, trying, falling, and trying again. Eventually, we master the process. Along the way, we learn a little more from every failure.
- **Don't dwell on your failures, dwell on your successes.** Maintaining a confident, positive attitude about yourself and what you are doing is critical, not only to your future performance, but to your personal happiness.

Avoiding failure is not the same as succeeding. There is no success without failure. And success and failure have the same root—the desire to achieve.

Remember, failure is a learning experience, an opportunity to try something new, and a necessary pathway to success.

All successful people learn to overcome failure. Learn from your failure: see it as a chance to try something new, and you can eventually view it as a necessary part of the road to success!

GO, GRANNY, GO!

Great-great-grandma gets high school diploma—at ninety-six

"Better late than never," quips Marjorie Bradshaw, who graduated from high school at the ripe old age of ninety-six!

Proudly wearing a blue cap and gown, the tiny great-great-grandmother—she's just 4-feet-11 inches—got out of her wheelchair, stepped up on stage, and got her diploma to the thunderous applause of the packed school auditorium in Bakersfield, California.

"My mother is a very determined woman," said daughter Pat Cantell, sixty-nine. "She sold products door-to-door until she was seventy-five. She took a computer class when she was well into her eighties. And she was still playing golf when she was ninety-two!

"She's a great example of what you can do if you're determined enough."

Marjorie was forced to drop out of high school at the start of her senior year in 1917 after her mother died. She was the oldest of seven children and was needed to look after the younger kids.

Twice widowed, she has three children, plus sixty-two grandchildren, great-grandchildren, and great-great-grandchildren. One of her granddaughters, Cindy Hurley, is a supervisor of special education at the local school district.

"Cindy asked me if I had any regrets," said Marjorie, "and I told her my only regret was that I had never graduated from high school. She said, 'Grandma, I think we can work on that.'"

Cindy contacted the Bakersfield Adult School and arranged for Marjorie to study at home.

"She would read the books and answer the questions," said Pat Cantell. "She tape-recorded her answers because her arthritis makes writing difficult, and Cindy would transcribe them."

"It wasn't difficult for her to study. She has cataracts and has to wear glasses, and she has hearing aids in both ears. But her mind is very sharp."

After a year's study, Marjorie got her diploma—eighty years after she was forced to drop out of school.*

* This story is retold with permission from the *National Enquirer.*

Step 2

Are You Ready for Change?

A setback is a clue—a symptom telling you that something isn't working and needs to be changed. That's why the aftermath of a failure is the best time to take stock of yourself and your situation to determine whether change is necessary.

Successful people make things happen. By contrast, those who fall behind are people who resist change or wait for someone else to change, complaining all the while!

IF YOU ALWAYS DO WHAT YOU'VE ALWAYS DONE, YOU'LL ALWAYS GET THE SAME RESULT.

I don't know who said this first, but whoever it was deserves a medal. Think about it: The people who accomplish the most are those who anticipate the need for change and then change *before* they have to.

The opposite is also true. Those who seem to be in trouble most of the time are guilty of not changing until it's too late—

until competitors have taken over, technology has passed them by, key people have resigned, and so on.

The skills required to anticipate the need for change are not complicated. The process is simple. It is based on the way our minds combine ideas to create new ones.

First Law for Growth: "Refocus quickly."

Solutions and new ideas are created by refusing to be limited by old ideas or experiences or by manipulating them. We combine them in new ways, put them in a new context of time or place, add other ideas, take something away, or change their meaning or purpose. Sometimes this process may take place accidentally and unconsciously. But to be a real change agent, we must do it deliberately and consciously. Charles Goodyear, for example, discovered the process of vulcanization when he tossed a batch of rubber he was mixing in a hot stove to hide it from his wife.

Too many people fear change. They cling to the familiar old shoe even if it cuts off circulation to their toes.—Wally "Famous" Amos

The bedrock question is, what is the process of using our experience to produce *new* ideas or to solve *new* problems?

Here are eight suggested steps:

1. **Name the target.** What's the problem? What kind of idea do you need?
2. **Get the facts.** Pile up all the information you can about the problem. This should include information about

unsuccessful attempts to solve it. Often ideas that failed one time will, with a slight change, succeed at another time.

3. **Try the obvious solutions first.** Often, merely naming a problem and collecting data about it will suggest solutions.
4. **Next: Try the wild ideas.** In particular, look for the apparently trivial, irrelevant aspects of the problem.
5. **Think intensely about the problem.** This is not really a separate step, but part of the steps already mentioned. Make yourself think about the problem until you have a solution or until you've reached what might be called a state of frustration.

The more we memorize, the less we think.

6. **Walk away from the problem.** Put it out of your conscious mind. At this point, if you have completed steps one through five, your subconscious will usually take over.
7. **Seize the flash of insight.** Generally, at some indefinite time after you walk away from the problem, you will find an answer welling up in your mind. Seize the idea at that moment and put it on paper.
8. **Do something about the idea.** Above all, don't give up. Most of us tend to get discouraged too easily. There are really easy ways to have good ideas, to solve tough problems. In the pursuit of an idea, the odds are all in favor of running into periods of discouragement when nothing goes right, when it appears that the answers will never come, when you begin to doubt the wisdom of what you are doing.

Results will not change before people do.

History is full of people who, through sheer determination, hung on through such periods—the Wright brothers, Alexander Graham Bell, Samuel Morse, Thomas Edison. Sam Walton is a more recent and very good example. In my books *Nobody Gets Rich Working for Somebody Else* and *If They Can—You Can: Lessons From America's New Breed Of Successful Entrepreneurs,* I summarize the success stories of over 350 living Americans. One of my most significant conclusions is that anyone who wants to try something new must go through disappointment and times when it seems much wiser to give up.

We resent change because it is risky, but to succeed in our professional lives, we simply must take risks. To wait for others is to fall behind. We must move forward even when:

- Other people hesitate to criticize our new ideas, or they say what they think we want to hear rather than reveal their true feelings.
- Urgency is stimulating unreliable judgments.
- Personal conflicts are working against a constructive, cooperative solution.
- Those who are responsible for creating a problem have become self-protective.
- People refuse to see a situation from any viewpoint but their own.
- Distasteful situations have created tension, fear, uncertainty, or even hostility.

OVERCONFIDENCE . . . The first words uttered by General George Custer upon spotting the Indians at Little Big Horn: "Hooray, boys, we've got 'em!"

Occasionally, everyone in a group will get along famously. In this situation, the dangers are:

- The group may use rationalizations instead of taking corrective action.
- Instead of seeking innovative ideas or quality decisions, the group may take the easy way out and fall back on loyalty or "safe" alternatives as a way to work the company through a problem.
- Polarization may occur between those for and those against the group's decisions. This is very difficult to deal with because you can be accused of playing favorites no matter which side you take.

The only way to win is to prepare to win.

WHAT DO YOU NEED TO CHANGE?

The most effective people are able to take inventory of their qualifications, especially when a new challenge arises.

How do you rate yourself in the following areas?

Self-Esteem

- Do you see yourself as valuable, worthy, and capable?
- Do you believe you can change and control the conditions that will lead to your success?

Responsibility

- Have you put into motion the events that will result in success?
- Do you acknowledge your accountability for both your successes and your failures?

Optimism

- Do you *believe* that your future will be good, productive, and profitable?

Goal Orientation

- Do you continually keep your goals before you and allow them to motivate you and direct your behavior?

Imagination

- Do you habitually imagine new and beneficial situations before they occur?

Awareness

- Are you alert to what's going on around you and aware of new opportunities that can help you meet your goals?

Creativity

- Are you *certain* there's a better way to do just about everything?

Communication

- Do you recognize that your success is rooted largely in your ability to get ideas across to others and to understand what others are saying to you?

Growth Orientation

- Do you give high priority to getting ready for your future?
- Do you welcome an opportunity to trade old, unproductive habits for new, profitable ones?

Response to Pressure

- Does pressure trigger constructive responses so you "peak up" rather than "cop out" when hostile conditions occur?

Outlook

- Is your energy contagious?
- Do others pick up your enthusiasm and begin to work with more enjoyment and involvement?

Risk-Taking

- Are you ready and willing to take reasonable risks?
- Are you committed to the idea that your goal is excellence, not perfection?

Immediacy

- Do you make decisions and take actions immediately, not because you *need* to but because you *want* to?
- Do you reflect a sense of power, motion, accomplishment, enthusiasm, and competence?

When you're through changing, you're through.—Bruce Barton

If you can answer these questions positively, you can feel comfortable about your future, because these are the qualities common to most high-performing people.

A number of negative answers may be a warning sign that your career is in need of renewal. To find out, ask yourself these revealing questions:

	Yes	No	Not Sure
1. Have I recently been passed over for a promotion?	☐	☐	☐
2. Have my salary increases been regular and commensurate with the company average?	☐	☐	☐
3. Have I recently received severe criticism from my boss?	☐	☐	☐
4. Is the turnover among my staff above average?	☐	☐	☐
5. Am I no longer invited to attend meetings I used to attend?	☐	☐	☐
6. Do things seem to be more "strained" at work?	☐	☐	☐
7. Are my coworkers beginning to avoid me?	☐	☐	☐
8. Do my superiors seem to be uncomfortable in my presence?	☐	☐	☐
9. Are there several "problem" people in my department?	☐	☐	☐
10. Have people stopped coming to me for suggestions or assistance?	☐	☐	☐

The proper answer to each of these questions, of course, is "no." A "not sure" is as bad as a "yes." If you have even one "yes" or "not sure" on the list, you're definitely due for a career tune-up. If you have two or three, your career may be in jeopardy already. And if you have more than three, it is entirely possible that your very job may be in danger. Carelessness with your career is as foolish as carelessness with your health. My advice is the same as that of your family physician:

- Undergo periodic check-ups.
- Take immediate steps to correct any deficiencies that may be discovered.

Fortunately, no particular "science" is required to heal an ailing career. If you are truly honest in conducting a self-evaluation, it is not difficult to determine where your strengths—and weaknesses—lie. And if you then make a conscientious effort to strengthen those skills associated with whatever area of weakness you find, the "cure" will almost always be effective.

Some of the sources from which self-improvement assistance may be obtained include:

- High school, college, or correspondence courses. (Many companies will pay part or all of your fees.)
- Business publications (including those that are published for people *outside* your own specialized industry).
- Books, audiocassettes and videotapes (many of which may be available at your public library).
- Specialized seminars offered by trade associations and similar groups.
- In-house training programs that may be offered by your Human Resources or Training and Development Department.

You may find that you do not, in fact, need extensive outside training. The awareness that a weakness exists may be sufficient to bring about a modification in your business behavior. For example, simply *recognizing* that you have not been as good a listener as you should be could easily result in a more dedicated and consistent effort to improve communications. That, in itself, could reduce a problem that has been hampering your progress.

DECISION-MAKING: THE ABILITY TO CREATE CHANGE

Good managers know that decision-making goes with the territory. Managers *must* make decisions!

Even if you are not a manager, the ability to make clear decisions is vital to your success. The ability to anticipate change is one-half of the recipe for success. The other half is the ability to decide to do something about it!

Use the following test to determine your Decision-Making Index (DMI):

Test Your Decision-Making Index (DMI)

	Never	Rarely	Occasionally	Often
1. Do you let the opinions of others influence your decisions?	☐	☐	☐	☐
2. Do you procrastinate when it's time to make a decision?	☐	☐	☐	☐
3. Do you let others make your decisions for you?	☐	☐	☐	☐
4. Have you missed out on an opportunity because you couldn't make a decision?	☐	☐	☐	☐

	Never	Rarely	Occasionally	Often
5. Do you tend to study so many details that it's hard to reach a decision?	☐	☐	☐	☐
6. After reaching a decision, do you tend to have second thoughts?	☐	☐	☐	☐
7. Did you hesitate while answering these questions?	☐	☐	☐	☐

Score one point for each *often,* two for each *occasionally,* three points for each *rarely,* and four points for each *never.*

If you scored 25–28, you are very decisive and probably have no problem assuming responsibility for the choices that you make.

If you scored 15–24, decision-making is difficult for you. You need to work at being more decisive.

If you scored 14 or below, you're going to have big problems unless you learn to overcome your resistance to change. When a change is needed, face up to it and do it!

When all is said and done, effectiveness requires *both* anticipation of when to change and a willingness to do it without flinching, before a crisis occurs.

Change is the price of survival.—Gary Player

DOES YOUR COMPANY NEED TO CHANGE?

The most successful people are those who aren't surprised very often. Let's face it—the same is true for companies. Employers who prepare for the future prosper. Those who bog down in outdated methods or worn out ideas will never be competitive.

But how can we get out of our ruts? Can inner change be forced? Can we really anticipate results accurately? If so, how? Where do we start?

The **Change Requirement Inventory (CRI)** below provides powerful clues about whether a company will be competitive in the twenty-first century. Think carefully about how you would rate your company in each category. If you don't soon see evidence of significant improvement in every area you now believe is weak, you should be very concerned about your future.

Change Requirement Inventory (CRI)

Weak companies will be: (1–5 points)	Strong companies will be: (5–10 points)	Rating (1–10)
Focused on the *company's* goals.	Focused on *customer* needs.	
Locked into separate departments.	Effective in groups and teams.	
Rewarding seniority.	Rewarding only performance.	
Compensating for credentials.	Compensating for results.	
Hiring quickly.	Thoroughly testing and investigating every new hire.	
Accepting most candidates.	Testing for attitude.	
Ignoring track record.	Insisting on accountability.	
Responding to direction from above.	Pushing decision-making down.	

Change Requirement Inventory (con't.)

Weak companies will be: (1–5 points)	Strong companies will be: (5–10 points)	Rating (1–10)
Writing new rules.	Creating new ways.	
Avoiding customer feedback.	Maintaining continuing contact.	
Ignoring customer input.	Measuring retention/ satisfaction rate continuously.	
Behind in using technology.	Updating technological solutions regularly.	
Available to customers during working hours.	Accessible around the clock.	
Retaining mediocre people.	Keeping only performers.	
Allowing unmeasurable judgments.	Evaluating objectively.	
Dictating methods.	Negotiating options.	
Setting strict boundaries.	Brainstorming ideas.	
Protecting incompetence.	Releasing ineffective people promptly.	
Rigidly controlling.	Pressing for self direction.	
Placing blame.	Making individuals accountable.	
Punishing mistakes.	Praising accomplishments.	
Stressful.	Enjoyable.	

Change Requirement Inventory (con't.)

Weak companies will be: (1–5 points)	Strong companies will be: (5–10 points)	Rating (1–10)
Avoiding investment in training.	Increasing training, mentoring, and coaching.	
Playing it safe.	Carefully selecting risks.	
Using people as expense.	Viewing people as assets.	
Faking that they care.	Meeting commitments.	
Layered from top down.	Networked throughout.	
Inbred and slow.	Opportunistic.	
Rigid.	Flexible.	
Penalizing risk takers.	Rewarding creativity.	
	Total	

This analysis will also be very helpful to vendors, suppliers, and customers. It will enable them to determine whether their relationships will be short-term or long-term. It will provide insight into the potential payoff of their investment of time, effort, and money.

The **Change Requirement Inventory (CRI)** can be effectively used in an evaluation format. Simply enter a company name and rate it in all thirty categories. Use a 1 (lowest) to 10 (highest) scale. Weak companies should be rated 1–5. Strong companies should be rated 6–10. Total ranking key:

Under 120 points	Unlikely to be competitive in 21st century.
120–240 points	Will need to change soon.
240 points or more	A good bet to succeed.

Start with an analysis of your own organization, and you will be much better equipped to evaluate others.

Once you have analyzed your organization, you will be in a better position to judge whether your outlook towards change is compatible with that of your employer. It's an important clue. If your company comes out on the weak side and you're looking for a long-term opportunity, a change in employers may be appropriate. After all, you don't want to devote your most productive years to an outfit making buggy whips!

Overcoming Conventional Wisdom Is Never Easy . . .

For centuries, people believed that Aristotle was right when he said that the heavier an object, the faster it would fall to earth. Aristotle was regarded as the greatest thinker of all time, and surely he could not be wrong. All it would have taken was for one brave person to take two objects, one heavy and one light, and drop them from a great height to see whether or not the heavier object landed first. But no one stepped forward until nearly two thousand years after Aristotle's death. In 1589, Galileo summoned learned professors to the base of the Leaning Tower of Pisa. Then he went to the top and pushed off a ten-pound weight and a one-pound weight. Both landed at the same time. But the power of belief in the conventional wisdom was so strong that the professors denied what they had seen. They continued to say Aristotle was right.

Tough Days . . .

Attorney-General Edwin Meese recalled the advice of his predecessor, William French Smith. The outgoing attorney-general warned Meese that there would be many a day when he would feel like "the javelin competitor who won the toss of the coin and elected to receive."

THE TOP TEN LIST FROM EMPLOYEE APPRAISALS

I haven't sent these to David Letterman yet, but I think they might merit mention! Have you met any of these people as employers, bosses, or coworkers?

10. "Since my last report, this employee has reached rock bottom and doesn't have a rope."
9. "People would follow him anywhere, but only out of morbid curiosity."
8. "This employee is really not so much of a has-been, but more of a definitely won't be."
7. "Works well when under constant supervision and cornered like a rat in a trap."
6. "When she opens her mouth, it seems that this is only to change whichever foot was previously in there."
5. "He would be out of his depth in a parking lot puddle."
4. "This young lady has delusions of adequacy."
3. "He sets low personal standards and then consistently fails to achieve them."
2. "This employee should go far, and the sooner he starts, the better."
1. "This employee is depriving a village somewhere of an idiot."

Whether you think you can or think you can't—you are right.—Henry Ford

TIMELESS, TRUSTWORTHY TENETS FOR EVERYDAY LIVING

Practically anywhere you turn these days you can hear someone say, "Why does everything have to be so complicated?" Well maybe, just maybe, we're guilty of making our lives more complex than they need to be. Perhaps the real culprit is controllable if we live by some simple rules. These, I believe, will make a big difference:

1. **Show up on time.** If you are chronically late, you take two big risks. First, you may miss the most important thing that happened; second, you may never catch up to the group.
2. **Listen.** It is no accident that God gave us one mouth and two ears. When we fail to listen, we shut off fully half of our learning potential.
3. **Never hide the truth.** Lies dig deep holes. Recovering from mistrust always takes more energy than consistently being honest.
4. **Don't look back.** Only historians have a legitimate need to look backward more than forward.
5. **Avoid unhealthy choices.** How many people do you know whose lives are complicated by poor health because they deliberately continue to make unhealthy choices? It's many more than the number traceable to accidents or unknown causes, isn't it?
6. **Be accountable.** The most important ability is accountability. *Nothing* happens until someone steps forward and says, "I'll do it."

7. **Don't make excuses.** Reputation does not crash, it crumbles. The more you make excuses, the more you are likely to believe them.
8. **Deliver what you promise.** Without honesty, there is no trust. Without trust, there is no confidence. Without confidence, there is no progress.
9. **Don't try to be perfect.** More is lost by waiting for perfection than by steadily moving forward.
10. **Change before you must.** Remember the six words that altered the face of the earth: "But, Noah, it isn't even raining"?

Step 3

Are You Convincing?

The best attitude in the world, the healthiest outlook in the world, the noblest intentions in the world—all are relatively useless unless they can be interpreted and conveyed convincingly.

No one can read your mind!

You can't make things happen until you can make others understand what you want to do and why.

Resilience and recovery require effective communication. Use this step to:

- pinpoint the assets and liabilities of your communication style,
- take action on these strong points and weak points,
- incorporate basic listening and questioning techniques into your daily work until they become habitual and are practiced routinely.

By taking steps to enhance your ability to communicate, you can get your message across better and bounce back quickly.

GETTING YOUR MESSAGE ACROSS

Communication is as much desire as it is technique. Where conversation is involved, for example, it must have purpose. It should be constructive and should recognize that the problems and questions others raise are *always* important to them.

Tact is the ability to tell someone where to go in such a way that they look forward to the trip.

To come across effectively to listeners and gain their cooperation, try:

- **Sharing information** quickly, while it's still fresh.
- **Focusing attention** on what the topic means personally to your listeners.
- **Being generous** in sharing viewpoints. *Examples:* "Are you comfortable with that?" "What is your reaction?"
- **Avoiding the** compulsion to do everything yourself. Delegate when possible, but keep the lines of communication open so you can follow up on what you've delegated.
- **Talking to** your people in a down-to-earth manner.

Communication is more than just talk. Listening carefully and then asking pertinent questions gets the information needed for orderly mental processing.

If you tell the truth, you don't have to remember anything.—Mark Twain

When you listen with care, it's possible to learn what options exist—especially those not immediately apparent. Listen for the facts, but listen at the same time for *why* you're being given this information. It's impossible to learn what is on someone else's mind when *you* are talking.

Effective leaders speak to hearts as well as minds.

HOW WELL DO YOU LISTEN?

While the value of good communication is widely recognized, the emphasis is usually on the giving end. But receiving—that is, listening—is just as important. The following questions will help you discover how well you listen. Try to answer each question honestly and objectively. Then score yourself and see where there is still some room for improvement.

When taking part in an interview or group conference, do you:

	Usually	Sometimes	Seldom
1. Prepare yourself physically by facing the speaker and making sure that you can hear?	☐	☐	☐
2. Watch the speaker as well as listen to him or her?	☐	☐	☐
3. Decide from the speaker's appearance and delivery whether what he has to say is worthwhile?	☐	☐	☐
4. Listen primarily for ideas and underlying feelings?	☐	☐	☐
5. Determine your own bias, if any, and try to allow for it?	☐	☐	☐
6. Keep your mind on what the speaker is saying?	☐	☐	☐

	Usually	Sometimes	Seldom
7. Interrupt immediately if you hear a statement you feel is wrong?	☐	☐	☐
8. Make sure before answering that you've taken in the other person's point of view?	☐	☐	☐
9. Try to have the last word?	☐	☐	☐
10. Make a conscious effort to evaluate the logic and credibility of what you hear?	☐	☐	☐

Score yourself as follows:
Questions 1, 2, 4, 5, 6, 8, 10
10 points for "usually"; 5 points for "sometimes; 0 for "seldom"
Questions 3, 7, 9
0 for "usually"; 5 points for "sometimes"; 10 points for "seldom"
Interpreting your score:
Above 90—You are a good listener.
75–90—Not bad, but you could improve
Below 75—You have problems as a listener.

Let your ideas seek words—never the reverse.

TO UNDERSTAND BETTER—TRY *LISTENING* BETTER

Listening is as important to communication as *speaking*. Whether the message is oral or written, it is not communicated properly unless the recipient understands its meaning fully and completely.

To become a better listener, it is necessary to:

- Show interest. Concentrate on the meaning of the words.
- Be understanding of the other person.
- Express empathy. Try to see yourself in their situation.
- Single out the problem, if there is one.

- Listen for specific causes of the problem.
- Help the speaker associate the problem with its causes.
- Encourage the speaker to develop competence and motivation to solve the problem independently.
- Cultivate the ability to be silent when silence is needed.

There are also several things a good listener should *not* do:

- Don't argue.
- Don't interrupt.
- Don't pass judgment too quickly or in anticipation of what the speaker has to say.
- Don't give advice unless it is requested.
- Don't jump to conclusions.

Listening is a key to *knowing* and *understanding.* One way to *know* more is to *listen* more and gather more information. A person's judgments and decisions are only as good as the information on which they are based.

Good leaders need to *listen* with greater intensity, *observe* with greater accuracy, *react to other people* with greater empathy, *really concentrate* on what they say, and *think and feel* with greater understanding.

The trouble with people who talk too much is that they often say things they haven't thought of yet.

IMPROVING LISTENING SKILLS

Much of your effectiveness rests on your ability to hear others out. To listen better, try these five time-tested steps:

- **Listen to clarify.** ("Do you mean . . . ?" "Is this the problem?")

- **Listen to check meaning and interpretation.** ("As I understand it, your plan is to . . ." "Your reasons for this decision are . . .")
- **Listen to be neutral.** ("I see." "Uh-huh." "That's interesting.")
- **Listen to show you understand.** ("You feel that . . ." "I gather you were rather surprised to learn that . . .")
- **Listen to bring a discussion into focus.** (These are the ideas you have mentioned . . ." "Your priorities are . . .")

Listening is a skill. Improving your listening ability doesn't require a vast stretch of your capabilities. It does demand your interest, common courtesy, patience, and willingness to learn. To begin:

- **Show your interest and understanding.** Strive for empathy.
- **Single out the problem** (if there is one) by listening carefully for its causes. Then help the speaker associate the problem with the causes by asking pertinent, open-ended questions. This frequently helps the speaker and others reach a solution to their problems.
- **Don't hog the limelight.** Good communicators don't try to hold a group spellbound. Rather, they skillfully draw others into the conversation.
- **Avoid interrupting,** judging too quickly or offering advice after hearing only a part of the story. Doing so can serve as a springboard for jumping to the wrong conclusions.
- **Stick to the point.** Often, people who feel they are expert in a particular field talk too much. Try to use as few words as possible.

The best way to be sure that you truly understand these techniques is to use them! My suggestion is that you incorporate them, one or two at a time, in ongoing job situations. You will be pleasantly surprised at how soon these techniques will "stick" and become routine.

Communication requires give and take. When you are listening to others, how you respond to what you are hearing can greatly enhance the communications process.

Some people will believe anything if you whisper it.

ASK THE RIGHT QUESTIONS

You're now aware of the need for good listening. But how about the importance of questioning?

The power of the question lies in the fact that *it compels an answer*. If we ask the *right* questions, we will get the right answers—in terms of information, experience, reactions, or other data we seek. If we ask the *wrong* questions, of course, we will get the wrong answers.

Asking has many advantages over telling. To manage effectively, you must have adequate information. Indeed, people's decisions are only as good as their information.

The higher people advance in the management hierarchy, the more they are removed from where the actual work is done. Consequently, they must rely more and more on oral and written communication—reports, memos, and the like. The usefulness of the information you get from others depends on the quality of the questions you ask.

Remember, it's crucial that you ask rather than tell. Remind yourself that because of experience, background, and training, each person can provide special information. Along with adopting this basic attitude and conviction, you need to:

- **Understand** the different *types* of questions—their nature, purpose, and use.
- **Know** how to channel and handle questions.
- **Develop** skill and proficiency in using questioning techniques in appropriate situations.

Following is a list of the basic types of questions and examples of each:

Questioning Techniques—Types of Questions

Types	Purpose	Examples
Factual	• To get information. • To open discussion.	• All the "W" questions: what, where, why, when, who—and how?
Explanatory	• To get reasons and explanations. • To broaden discussion. • To develop additional information.	• "In what way would this help solve the problem?" • "What other aspects of this should be considered?" • Just how would this be done?"
Justifying	• To challenge old ideas. • To develop new ideas. • To get reasoning and proof.	• "Why do you think so?" • "How do you know?" • "What Evidence do you have?"
Leading	• To introduce a new idea. • To advance a suggestion by you or others.	• "Should we consider this as a possible solution?" • "Would this be a feasible alternative?"

Types	Purpose	Examples
Hypothetical	• To develop new ideas. • To suggest another, possibly unpopular, opinion. • To change the course of the discussion.	• "Suppose we did it this way—what would happen?" • "Another company does this. Is this feasible here?"
Alternative	• To make a decision between alternatives. • To get agreement.	• "Which of these solutions is better, A or B?" • "Does this represent our choice in preference to . . . ?"
Coordinating	• To develop consensus. • To get agreement. • To take action.	• "Can we conclude that this is the next step?" • "Is there general agreement, then, on this plan?"

Ask the Right Question

A salesman stepped up on the porch of a house and rang the doorbell. Through the window, he could see into the living room, where a young boy was practicing the piano. Upon hearing the doorbell, the young pianist got up and answered the door. The salesman asked the boy, "Young man, is your mother home?" The kid looked at the salesman with a smirk on his face and replied, "Now, what do you think?"!

Questioning Techniques: Direction of Questions

Type	Purpose	Examples
A. Overhead: Directed to group	• To open discussion.	• "How shall we begin?" • "What should we consider next, anyone?" • "What else might be important?"
B. Direct: Addressed to a specific person.	• To call on someone for special. information. • To involve someone who has not been active.	• "Al, what would be your suggestions?" • Sue, have you had any experience with this?"
C. Relay: Referred back to another person or to the group.	• To help leader avoid giving own opinion. • To get others involved in the discussion. • To call on someone who knows the answer.	• "Would someone like to comment on Bill's question?" • "John, how would you answer Bill's question?"
D. Reverse: Referred back to person who asks question.	• To help leader avoid giving own opinion. • To encourage questioner to think himself/herself. • To bring out opinions.	• "Well, Linda, how about giving us your option first?" • "Bob, tell us first what your own experience has been?"

USING LISTENING AND QUESTIONING SKILLS TO GET GOOD INFORMATION

Whether you are self-employed or working in an organization, you simply must be able to elicit good information from others. Unreliable or untrustworthy information, or information from "false prophets" who have their own welfare in mind, can trigger a catastrophe. Poor information may be the reason you suffered a setback. When you are trying to recover, poor information may lead to a false start or another setback.

> **If everyone is thinking alike, then somebody isn't thinking.**—George S. Patton

How can you get high-quality information from other people to make fact-based decisions?

The gentle art of cross-examination in evaluating information is part of the job of problem-solving and decision-making. Before you accept information from someone else at face value, check the credibility of the source by asking yourself the following questions:

- Is the person generally reliable?
- Is the person in a good position to have learned what he or she is telling you?
- Does the person have a personal or organizational stake in the outcome?
- Is the person defending somebody else?
- Is the person a chronic optimist or pessimist, and what effect might this have on the information you receive?
- Does the information come from an emotionally charged atmosphere, and how might this affect the quality of the information?

- Could your informant simply be mistaken?
- Are you being drawn into an internal feud?
- Is somebody quibbling with the facts?
- Is anything being covered up?

EXPERIENCE COUNTS

Christopher Columbus was stranded in Jamaica and needed supplies. He knew that an eclipse was to occur the next day. He told the tribal chief, "The God who protects me will punish you. Unless you give me supplies this night, a vengeance will fall upon you and the moon shall lose its light." When the eclipse darkened the sky, Columbus got all the supplies he needed.

In the early 1900s, an Englishman tried the same trick on a Sudanese chieftain. "If you do not follow my order," he warned, "vengeance will fall upon you and the moon will lose its light." "If you are referring to the lunar eclipse," the Sudanese chieftain replied, "that doesn't happen until the day after tomorrow."

COMMUNICATING WITH YOUR BOSS

When you begin to communicate more effectively, more efficiently, and more clearly, all of your relationships will improve—especially your relationship with your boss.

Every conversation with your boss is important, whether you chat near the soda machine or sit down together for a lengthy discussion.

Consider how you actually speak to your boss. Are you quick to put your thoughts into words—a little too glib—or does it take you time to formulate your ideas? Hesitancy on your part can be construed as lack of knowledge, whereas responding too quickly can make you seem impulsive or abrupt and rude.

Above all, *think* before you speak, and practice putting your thoughts into words. It is important to say what is really on your mind!

Speak thoughtfully—words endure.

When the subject of your discussion requires a formal meeting, make an appointment to see your boss. One-to-one meetings with bosses are the most direct and focused type of communication. Regular meetings can build good rapport with your boss and may forge a relationship that can last when it's your turn to deliver bad news. The following guidelines will be helpful:

- Determine whether a meeting is necessary.
- Determine the objective of the meeting.
- Choose the time and place wisely.
- Organize your thoughts. Identify your purpose, the projected outcome, and what you want to communicate, so you will know exactly what you want to talk about.

Determining your objectives and defining the problem are two separate tasks. Before asking for a meeting with your boss, you need to clearly define the problem or issues you want to discuss. If your boss absorbs information better by reading, then prepare an outline or written summary.

During the meeting, pay attention to the nonverbal feedback you're getting from and giving to your boss. Stay focused and responsive. Afterwards, be sure to thank your boss for her time. Follow up with any necessary documentation such as summaries or performance agreements.

Solving Communication Problems

Sometimes communication between you and your boss goes awry. You may not be able to pinpoint what's wrong, but you sense that your boss is not giving you proper guidance to get the job done or that you aren't communicating well.

The key is to communicate concisely. Most bosses hate having to answer a series of unrelated questions or dealing with a problem in a piecemeal fashion. If that is the case, you should be assertive about getting a response. If your boss is always in the office at 7:30 A.M. or on weekends, grab a few minutes of his time then.

When communication breaks down, the fragile relationship between boss and employee can be irreparably damaged. The fault is rarely just one person's. As in marriages that falter, both partners in a working relationship contribute their share to the communication problem. If your boss is a good manager, he'll understand his responsibilities and take the initiative to prevent festering. When your boss won't attempt to solve a communication problem, however, it's in your best interest to take charge and start looking for solutions.

Communicating effectively is a lifelong pursuit. Missing skills can make or break any relationship on or off the job. At work, you will be better off if you learn the skills that will enable you to carry 60 percent of the communication load, leaving your boss only 40 percent. Once you accept that ratio, you will have fewer disappointments and many more successes.

THE ADVANTAGE OF DISADVANTAGE

In the early 1940s Charles Levy told John Johnson there was absolutely no way that Levy's Circulating Company could sell a magazine for blacks. There was just no market; nobody would read it. Undeterred, Johnson corralled dozens of friends to call Levy and ask for a publication called *Negro Digest.*

Weeks later, Levy conceded. "Maybe we've got something here," he said as he placed his first order for the much-requested *Negro*

Success and failure have the same root—desire to achieve. Avoiding failure is not the same as success.

Digest, which then somewhat miraculously sold out wherever it was placed.

Negro Digest became *Ebony.* Today, Johnson's company has annual revenues of nearly $362 million.

To get there, Johnson says, he simply practiced persistence and patience and "learned to take advantage of every disadvantage." For example, the friends who went from newsstand to newsstand asking for *Negro Digest* were the same ones to whom Johnson later slipped a couple of bucks to buy every copy of *Negro Digest* that Levy had originally put out for sale.

"I didn't have any money left, but it worked. The magazine had a distributor," Johnson told some six hundred Harvard Business School graduates.

Step 4

Can You Control Yourself?

People out of control can *never ever* be at their best. All of your assets blow up when you explode. People who cannot retain control of their emotions are risky investments. If everyone doubts your ability to capitalize on your strengths because of volatility, you will be trusted less and less in important situations. No one wants to advocate someone for higher responsibility if there is the slightest doubt that the individual will be a loose cannon!

This step will help you pinpoint the emotions you need to manage and will and provide techniques for doing so.

> **Fools are nourished by anger—**
> **wise men by self-control.**

MANAGING YOUR EMOTIONS

Emotions can be volatile or chilling. They can make us explode with anger or droop from depression. No matter what their nature, the effect of emotions on our energy is draining, whether it's through the volatile rush of a temper tantrum or gradual withdrawal because of guilt or fear.

It's best to know what kind of emotions you experience on a daily basis. See if any of the following statements describe you:

1. I hide or suppress my annoyance with others.
2. I am frequently bored.
3. I can't concentrate on my work.
4. I feel pressured from all directions.
5. I avoid involving others in decision-making and planning.
6. When I become angry, I feel guilty afterward.
7. I frequently worry about trivial matters.

If you answered "yes" to any of the questions above, you may have problems handling one or more of the six basic emotions: Anger, Depression, Joy, Trust, Fear, and Anxiety.

Everyone feels these emotions with some degree of intensity. They're only a problem when they keep us from performing our job—whether it's as a good employee, an effective parent or a happy and fulfilled adult.

Anger and Depression

Some emotions funnel naturally into others. Unexpressed anger can lead to depression; unexamined fear can result in a heightened level of anxiety. Your performance at work will improve—your whole life will improve—when you're aware of your feelings and know how to deal with them. If you answered "yes" to statements one and six above, you're experiencing anger.

Surprisingly, feelings are often controlled by thoughts. Negative thoughts lead to depression just as fearful thoughts lower self-esteem. Learning to monitor your negative thoughts is the first step to getting control of your emotions.

If you were to ask most people if they are angry, they would probably deny it. But here are some symptoms of unacknowledged anger:

- Tense, tight muscles.
- Speaking in a loud voice.
- Knot in stomach.
- Nervous mannerisms.
- Quick, shallow breathing.
- Increased heart rate.

> **When dealing with people, remember you are not dealing with creatures of logic, but creatures of emotion.**—Dale Carnegie

People can suppress anger and bottle it up or express it in uncontrolled outbursts; either way, anger is a particularly potent emotion. Unexpressed or poorly expressed anger can damage your relationships with others because they will sense your latent hostility and will feel defensive. You must decide whether to be its slave or master.

Your feelings of anger, particularly with your boss, might be justified. Perhaps you have a boss who likes to upset and frustrate employees deliberately. Take your "emotional temperature" and see if you have any unresolved feelings of anger toward your boss. Try to be objective and determine if they're justified. If so,

- Clearly point out to him what he's doing that causes your angry reactions.
- Suggest possibilities for change.

If he's unwilling to change his behavior, you should devise ways to check your own reactions before they reach the boiling point by:

- Excusing yourself for a cooling off period when discussions become heated.
- Staying in touch with your feelings and giving your boss feedback such as "It's difficult for me to follow your instructions when you yell."

If your angry feelings toward your boss, coworkers, or customers seem unjustified or out of proportion, chances are you're dealing with previously unresolved issues of anger. To find out if your anger is chronic, ask yourself:

- Do I lose my temper easily over trivial matters?
- Does my boss's behavior remind me of someone else with whom I'm really angry?
- Is my anger predictable, occurring at certain times of the day (after breakfast, after lunch) when blood sugar is low?

Find a professional who can help you deal with your anger. It could be getting in the way of your career. When your boss sees you as overly emotional and edgy, he'll hesitate to trust you with important assignments. As much as he values your strengths and abilities, your volatile, unpredictable reactions might make you an undependable team player.

Depression is a feeling of sadness or grief. It can spring from unexpressed anger or stem from a particular event such as illness, a death in the family, or a failure at work.

Depression has few, if any, positive effects. It does tell you something is wrong. When you deny depression, preferring not to examine its cause, it can turn into chronic depression, which lowers your energy level and makes you unable to function.

The most effective way to cure depression is to first identify what's causing it. That can be relatively simple if you are suffering from an isolated case of depression caused by a major change in your life (moving, divorce, illness, and the like).

However, if you are chronically depressed, identifying the source of your depression may be more difficult. This type of depression can be driven by numerous complex emotions. Among them are:

- Low self-esteem
- Feelings of insecurity
- Constant need for approval

If you think you fall into this category of chronic depression, consider talking to a counselor, psychologist, minister, or other professional who can help you identify and correct the source of your depression.

You may have the world's most empathetic boss, or you may not. But even a supportive boss gets tired of an employee who needs constant re-energizing to get the job done.

Joy and Trust

Joy is, or should be, a very real part of our daily lives both at home and at work. It restores our energies and regenerates our view of the world.

The effects of joy in the workplace are limitless. It can:

- Motivate employees to participate in consuming, goal-oriented work.
- Promote sharing, generosity, and teamwork.
- Allow employees to substitute the pleasures of discovery for the dull patterns of habit and routine.

Joy fuels you with added energy. It allows you to work hard, acting with confidence and decisiveness, pushing projects through to conclusion.

Without trust, the corporate world would no longer exist. It's the glue that binds all relationships and agreements. Your trust in others can be limited by how much you trust yourself. Self-trust gives you several distinct advantages on the job:

1. It allows you to recognize and rely on your abilities.

2. It gives you confidence to cope with difficult situations.
3. It provides you with the inner strength to act decisively and push for results that may lack popular support.

Mutual trust among employees and employers allows you to bypass time-consuming red tape, cumbersome rules and regulations. Once trust is established, both you and your boss will be more innovative, and your jobs will be more fun.

Fear and Anxiety

Fear is one of the most basic emotions known to man. It prompts the body to pump adrenaline in anticipation of the classic "fight or flight" situation. We experience fear almost daily, yet not many people would admit to being fearful. It simply doesn't go with the confident image demanded by the corporate world, yet we're all afraid of making mistakes, of displeasing our bosses, of losing our jobs.

Some people are afraid of not "fitting in"—of how business associates would regard them if they were to act slightly different, or if their true natures were known. Some of those who have made it to top-level management jobs suffer from the impostor syndrome: They have constructed a professional persona that conforms to others' expectations. They are actors and actresses.

A person in this situation may feel she has to be tough with her employees to appear strong, or that she must become a workaholic and forgo spending time with her family to conform to a hard-driving executive image.

When fear goes unexamined, it can produce a high level of anxiety. Keep in mind that it's an emotion that won't simply go away. To deal with fear effectively, you must recognize it then control it to your advantage.

To overcome fear, it helps to rationally identify what you are afraid of, then think of a worst-case scenario. Make a realistic evaluation of what is liable to happen. Your list could look something like this:

- Fear: Making mistakes at work
- Effect: Being ridiculed

Worst possible outcome:
I become angry, lose control, lose coworkers' respect.
Realistic evaluation:
Everyone makes mistakes. Reasonable mistakes are generally tolerated where I work. I can learn from my mistakes.

Believe it or not, fear has positive uses in the business environment. It all depends on intensity and duration. Moderate, occasional fear stimulates; continuous fear paralyzes.

The best way to conquer fear is to learn to relax, visualize yourself in a positive situation, and make positive affirmations. Nothing can do more damage to your work performance than being afraid of your boss. You have to ask yourself if your fear is justified or misplaced. Does your boss bully and threaten employees, or does your insecurity with your boss's ego make you uneasy?

Unless your boss is violent, vindictive, or deviant, chances are she's testing to see how far you will let her go with her "obnoxious boss act." If you think your boss's bark is worse than her bite, stand up to her. Fear of your boss may be the major hurdle you must overcome. Tell her how her behavior makes you feel and that you'd prefer she monitor it when you're around. She might not change, but may respect you for having the nerve to confront her.

If, however, her bite is worse than her bark, you've got a tough boss to handle.

Anxiety produces feelings of uneasiness and apprehension. Anxiety can result when you are worrying about a future event rather than confronting a present danger. Many people experience anxiety in stress-related situations like these:

- Time pressures to work more quickly.
- Evaluation of your work by your boss.
- Increasing demands or complexity of your job.
- Learning new skills.
- Health problems.
- Inner conflicts between personal values and job responsibilities.
- Coming into contact with a large number and/or variety of people.
- Getting a new job or a new boss.

People experience anxiety when they have to make changes. However, many times these changes are positive. Anxiety can have effects in the workplace. It can, for instance:

- Motivate you to attack a problem directly.
- Help you analyze a situation.
- Prompt you to set goals, reevaluate your talents and abilities, and so on.

In addition, you may have to learn a few more skills to decrease your anxiety level, such as becoming more assertive or learning relaxation techniques.

No boss likes to work with a worrywart. If your boss perceives you as being overly concerned with petty details or taking up his time whining and complaining, her trust in you will erode.

When your anxiety is justified—due to unconfirmed rumors, or the company's poor financial performance—ask your boss to verify your information. She may not be in a position to confirm or deny the bad news, but she'll appreciate your letting her in on the grapevine.

To Gain Control of Your Emotions . . .

- Learn to monitor your negative thoughts.
- Take your emotional temperature, and see if you have any unresolved feelings of anger toward your boss.
- Consider finding a professional to help you deal with anger or depression.
- Take steps to boost your self-esteem and build your self-trust.
- Think of a worst-case scenario and a more realistic evaluation for each of your fears in the workplace.
- Keep a diary of your emotions, and watch for patterns that you can learn to control.

MANAGING STRESS

Stress is part of daily life, but it can become a serious obstacle. Driving in heavy traffic can produce stress; so can winning a marathon. Many Type-A high achievers find pleasure in the slight buzz they experience from so much to do in so little time. It's important to remember that stress can be caused by too many problems or by too much success. Either way, your body interprets it as an overload of stimuli and responds by telling the adrenals to kick into high gear.

Defining Overload

Stress, when handled improperly, can quickly escalate through various stages, beginning with anxiety and ending in a total inability to function. At this stage, stress is your body's way of "just saying no"—and it means it.

Stress in the workplace often occurs when you take on too much. You feel it's your job to solve not only your own problems but those of your boss and staff as well. Your overloaded schedule may not kill you, but it can put a damper on your overall outlook on life. A life that is devoted to work—with no time for fun or relaxation—can put you into a state of exhaustion and depression.

Look at what you do. Evaluate how stressful your job is. Unresolved emotional conflicts or poor time management can also add to your level of stress.

To assess the built-in stress of your position, you need to pin down your own answers to the following questions:

- Is my job stressful within itself (that is, is there high pressure to perform, to meet deadlines)?
- Do I make it more stressful than it needs to be?
- Does my boss make it more stressful than it needs to be?
- Do I have any personal power in this position?
- How many bosses must I please?
- Am I meeting overall goals in this position?

What to Do If Overwork Becomes a Problem

As downsized corporations delegate more work to fewer people, many employees are spending, fifty, sixty, even seventy hours a week handling a workload that was once spread among a group of people.

If your company has downsized without reducing the overall workload, your efforts to meet unrealistic expectations about your productivity may wear you out.

These expectations may not all come from your boss. In downsized companies, chances are good that *everyone* is struggling to keep up, your boss included. Time management tactics—such as setting priorities, eliminating routine but time-consuming activities, and delegating what you can—will help you keep your head above the water.

But there are other steps you can take to make sure that overwork does not push you over the edge.

- Monitor your stress level and stay alert for signs of stress such as irritability, poor concentration, or depression.
- Find a sympathetic ear who knows what you're going through.
- Add a little fun to your life by treating yourself to short, enjoyable activities several times a day. Take a few minutes to call a friend, walk around the block, pull up the solitaire game on your computer, or solve a few crossword puzzle clues.

The Good, The Bad, and The Ugly

Not all stress is bad. Some people bask in the glow of a high-pressure but rewarding working environment. See if you recognize any of the following examples of "good" stress:

- Passion and enthusiasm for your work.
- Being centered in the present, refusing to dwell on past successes or failures.
- Resourcefulness: drawing upon your ability to accomplish goals and create solutions constructively and imaginatively.
- Perseverance: a commitment to innovation.
- Optimism: an openness to new options.
- Goal setting: defining specific goals to be accomplished within specific time frames.

How Stress Affects Your Relationship With Your Boss

Even if you and your boss see eye-to-eye, stress can still affect your working relationship. See if any of the following situations fit:

- Your boss loads you down with plenty to do, but after you've met tough deadlines he fails to recognize your accomplishments.
- Your boss increases your responsibilities, but doesn't give you the resources (position or staff) to accomplish them.
- Your boss explains that you need to manage time more effectively, then derails you in a series of lengthy, pointless meetings.

"Joyless" stress comes from feeling disenfranchised, powerless, and overburdened with detailed tasks. Sometimes, to gain more control of your life, you must say "no" to a demanding or dictatorial boss. It can also make you better able to interact with your boss when he realizes that you will not tolerate unreasonable demands.

It is your responsibility to see how you and your boss create stress for one another. Is it "good" stress or "bad" stress? How much of it is avoidable through better planning, better communication?

It's surprising how often people will agree with you if you just keep your mouth shut.

REDUCING STRESS

Dealing with stress means learning to improve coping skills. Stress comes less from the environment than from the way we react to it.

The medical community says between one-half and three-quarters of routine medical practice is devoted to treating people with some complaint directly related to their stress response.

Stress can affect almost everybody. Have you noticed these symptoms in yourself, your coworkers, employees, or boss?

1. **Reduced clarity** of judgment and effectiveness.

2. **Rigid** behavior.
3. **Medical** problems.
4. **Strained relationships** with others because of irritability.
5. **Increasingly frequent** absences.
6. **Emerging addictive** behaviors (for example, drugs, alcohol, smoking).
7. **Expressions of** inadequacy and low self-esteem.
8. **Apathy** or anger on the job.

Identify and create the right blend of work and play.

Manage Stress by Taking Time Out

As society grows more complex, playtime activities are emerging as a way to cope. Psychologists agree that play and leisure activities serve as necessary mental "downtime" to regroup and bounce back from daily pressures.

It's important to identify and to create the right blend of work and play.

Some time should be spent in free-time activities that allow you to enjoy yourself. Examples are solitary bicycle rides, walks in the park, reading, and writing.

After solitary play comes group play. Make it a point to interact with friends at least once a week.

Vacations allow you to leave worries behind without feeling guilty. Psychologists are beginning to believe what employees have known for years: One week of vacation may not be enough.

Effective free time is characterized by the following principles: It must be *positive* to have a longer-lasting, uplifting effect; it must be mentally *purposeful* to facilitate coping with life's stresses; and, most of all, it must be *playful* so that life will continue to be spontaneous and exciting.

If you let it get to you, it will.

WHO FINISHES FIRST?

There is a popular misconception that pushy, stubborn, or belligerent people don't get ahead in their work and that "only nice people finish first."

It's hard to understand where that idea came from. There are too many exceptions in every workplace.

People "get ahead" because they *produce.* If you are hard to get along with, if you are antagonistic, self-centered, rude, and generally obnoxious. . . but you produce . . . you will probably still get ahead. And a lot of "nice" people will shake their heads and wonder how it ever happened.

Meanwhile, many of those "nice" people may be so busy trying to please, trying to win friends and influence people that they never get their work done. They have failed to produce. And when they fail to produce, they will *never* get ahead, no matter how popular they may be.

We've all seen examples:

- The person who's never too busy to listen when you talk about your summer vacation.
- The group of people who would never miss their midmorning coffee break together.
- The person who's always busy . . . doing something for the church, or the club, or a neighbor, but not for work.

These are "nice" people . . . but they seldom get ahead. Promotions should not go to the most *popular* individuals, but to the most *productive* individuals.

Many have learned to be both popular *and* productive, which definitely is to their advantage, but you can bet that they didn't attain their success as the result of a personality poll. They did it by *out-performing*, not *out-smiling* their associates.

Success is attained by recognizing the objectives of the company, by setting high standards of achievement, and by meeting those goals consistently.

Failure is determined in large part by what we allow to happen—Success by what we make happen.

Step 5

Is Time on Your Side?

Precious Time

Time is your most precious resource. How you use it will determine the quality of your life. Do you take time to:

- **Think:** It is the source of self-renewal.
- **Play:** It will keep you young.
- **Read:** It will rejuvenate your mind.
- **Worship:** It is the acknowledgment of your limitations.
- **Help needy people:** It will return more than you give.
- **Show love:** It is the key to life's greatest satisfactions.
- **Daydream:** It will provide a road map for your future.
- **Laugh:** It restores your balance.
- **Work on new skills:** It will keep you in demand.
- **Plan:** It will determine whether you have time for everything you want to do.

When I misuse time, I have wasted the only resource I can never restore.

Are You Time-Conscious?

Unless you cultivate respect for time and are continually conscious of its passage, you are apt to waste it. Ask yourself the following questions and determine how time-sensitive you are.

1. Do you know how much one hour of your time is worth?
2. Is your day's schedule of activities firmly in your mind when you arrive at the office?
3. Do you have a fairly accurate idea of what you ought to get done this week? This month? This quarter?
4. Have you delegated as much work as possible?
5. Do you weigh the time requirements of various tasks before assigning them to others or undertaking them yourself?
6. Do you wade into high-priority, tough, and unpleasant jobs rather than devoting too much time to things you like to do?
7. Do you carry a notebook with you for jotting down ideas, information, insights, and so on, rather than relying on your memory?
8. Do you use modern technology to save time—for example, personal computers, E-mail, fax machines, conference calls, and the like?
9. Do you know how to screen visitors and phone calls?
10. Is there a steady flow of clear communication between you and your coworkers?
11. Do you consciously appraise—and police—your use of leisure time?
12. Have you developed routine ways of handling routine matters?
13. When things are going well, do you take advantage of the momentum by tackling other tough chores, or do you ease off?
14. Do you challenge the way things are done because you think

there is always a more efficient way to get things done?

15. Do you have some "fill-in" jobs in case you suddenly find some spare time (for example, a broken appointment)?

Three or more "no's" suggest it's time to change your ways!

What's Your Time Worth?

Based on 244 eight-hour working days a year, the following eye-opening chart will tell you the true value of your time:

Annual Salary	Every Minute is Worth	Every Hour is Worth	One Hour a Day Annually is Worth
$ 8,000	$ .0683	$ 4.10	$ 1,000
10,000	.0854	5.12	1,249
12,000	.1025	6.15	1,500
15,000	.1280	7.68	1,875
20,000	.1708	10.25	2,500
25,000	.2135	12.81	3,125
35,000	.2988	17.93	4,375
40,000	.3416	20.50	5,000
50,000	.4268	25.61	6,250
$1,000,000	$8.523	$512.30	$125,000

As the chart makes clear, when you waste time you are also wasting money. What are your time-wasting habits?

- Doing everything yourself?
- Worrying about problems?
- Participating in endless meetings?
- Writing reports or letters longhand?
- Procrastinating?
- Engaging in long-winded conversations?
- Coping with recurring emergencies?

Whatever your time-wasting habits may be, there's help and hope for you. Now it's time to take a close look at one of your days. Follow the instructions carefully.

SAVING TIME WITH A DAILY TIME LOG

A Daily Time Log is presented on the following two pages. To use if effectively, follow these directions:

A. List date and goals for the day in terms of results, not activities. For example, "Complete agenda within time allocated for sales meetings," rather than "Hold sales meetings."

B. Record all significant acts in terms of results during each fifteen-minute period. DO NOT WAIT until noon or the end of the day, when the benefit is lost.

C. Upon completion, immediately answer the questions that follow the log.

Daily Time Log

Date ______________________

Goals: 1. ______________ 2. ______________ 3. ______________

4. ______________ 5. ______________ 6. ______________

Time	Action	Priority	Comment/Disposition/Results
		1=Important & Urgent 2=Imp.—Not Urgent 3=Urgent—Not Imp. 4=Routine	Delegate to ____________. Train ____________ to handle. Next time ask for recommendation. Next time say "No." Consolidate/Eliminate/Cut Time. Other.
8:00			
8:30			
9:00			
9:30			
10:00			
10:30			
11:00			

Time	Action	Priority	Comment/Disposition/Results
11:30			
12:00			
12:30			
1:00			
1:30			
2:00			
2:30			
3:00			
3:30			
4:00			
4:30			
5:00			
5:30			
Evening			

Questions

1. Did setting daily goals and times for completion improve your effectiveness? Why or why not? ______________________________

____

2. What was the longest period of time without interruption? ____

____

3. In order of importance, which interruptions were most costly? __

____

4. What can be done to eliminate or control them? ____________

____

5. Which telephone calls were unnecessary? ________________

____

6. Which telephone calls could have been shorter or more effective?

____

7. Which visits were unnecessary?______________________

8. Which visits could have been shorter or more effective? ______

____

9. How much time was spent in meetings? ________________

10. How much was necessary? _________________________

11. How could more have been accomplished in less time? ______

12. Did you tend to record "activities" or "results"? ____________

13. How many of your daily goals contributed directly to your long-range goals and objectives?______________________________

14. Did a "self-correcting" tendency appear as you recorded your actions? What two or three steps could you now take to improve your effectiveness? ______________________________

Ever notice that the person with an hour to kill wants to spend it with someone who can't spare a minute?

INTERCEPT THOSE INTERRUPTIONS!

Try the following solutions to reclaim some of your valuable time.

A. Visitors—Unscheduled and Scheduled

Problems	Solutions
1. The feeling that it's important to be asked for advice or to have social drop-ins	Recognize. Be available at lunch.
2. Desire to keep informed, to stay on the grapevine	Accomplish this on a planned, more certain basis.
3. Fear of offending	Be tactful but firm. Take time to log and carefully assess number and impact of all interruptions.
4. Ineffective screening techniques	Train secretary to screen visitors and calls without offending.
5. Ineffective monitoring of visits (scheduled and unscheduled)	Have someone interrupt (by phone or in person) to remind you of approaching end of time available. Wrist alarm is self-reminder. Preset time limit on visitors; foreshadow end of visit. Log time scheduled for appointments, time actually spent, and reason for discrepancy (if any).
6. Making decisions below your level	Make only the decisions employees can't make.
7. Requiring or expecting employees to "check with you" excessively	Manage by exception.
8. Failure to delegate	Do nothing you can delegate.

	Problems on matters delegated should be taken to persons handling the matters.
9. Desire to socialize	Do elsewhere.
10. No plans for unavailability	Have a quiet hour; modified "open door" policy.
11. Encouraging staff to bring their problems to you	Don't encourage dependence and staff's dropping in with questions. Encourage initiative, risk-taking, decision-making.

B. Telephone

Problems	Solutions
1. No secretary	Have switchboard screen calls. Use cut-off switch.
2. The need to appear available	Have call-backs.
3. No plan	Reserve time to plan.
4. Enjoy socializing	Do it elsewhere.
5. Lack of self-discipline	Learn to use group calls.
6. The need to remain informed and involved	Meet key people frequently.
7. Poor screening	Train secretary to intercept and divert.
8. Ego	Recognize and control.
9. Misdirected calls	Train.
10. Unable to terminate	Be brief. Learn techniques: Egg timer. Say "Thanks for calling" or "I'm sorry, I have another call."
11. Uncertain of responsibilities	Clarify.
12. Fear of offending	Be tactful but firm.

Better three hours too early, than one minute too late.—William Shakespeare

C. Meetings

Problems	Solutions
1. Lack of purpose	Call no meetings without a purpose. Have purpose in writing, if possible.
2. Lack of agenda	No meeting should be held without an agenda.
3. Wrong people/too many people	Have present only those who are needed.
4. Wrong time	Ensure opportune timing.
5. Wrong place	Select location consistent with objectives of meeting, freedom from interruptions, physical equipment necessary, minimum of travel for majority of people.
6. No planning	Allow for and schedule appropriate planning time.
7. Too many meetings	Test need for "regular" meetings. Occasionally don't hold it—see what happens. For meetings that tend to last too long, cut time allowed in half.
8. Inadequate motive	Provide written notice with all essentials, including expected contribution and materials necessary for preparation.
9. Not starting on time	Start on time. (By delaying for late arrivals, the leader penalizes those arriving on time and rewards those who come late!)
10. Socializing	Reserve socializing for more appropriate places. Get down to business.
11. Allowing interruptions	Set policy and let everyone know. Wherever possible,

Problems	Solutions
	allow no interruptions except for clear-cut emergencies. Take messages for delivery at coffee break and lunch time.
12. Wandering from agenda	Expect and demand adherence to agenda. Resist "hidden agenda" ploys.
13. Failure to set ending time for time allotments for each subject	Limit the time of the meeting and of each item on the agenda. Discussion time should correspond to importance of subject.
14. Failure to end on time	Do end on time, otherwise no one can plan for the time immediately following.
15. Indecision	Keep objective in mind and move toward it.
16. Deciding without adequate information	Ensure that requisite information will be available before convening meeting.
17. Failure to summarize conclusions and to record in minutes	Summarize conclusions to ensure agreement and remind participants of assignments. Record decisions, assignments, and deadlines in concise minutes. Distribute at least one day before meeting.
18. Failure to follow up	Ensure effective follow-up on all decisions. List uncompleted items under "unfinished business" at beginning of next agenda. Request status report until completed.
19. Failure to terminate committees when business or objectives are accomplished.	Take committee inventory. Abolish committees whose mission has been accomplished.

PLAN YOUR PROGRESS

As part of your personal time management, plan your progress.

Instructions: Complete the following statements. Mark your calendar so that in six months you will look at this page and see how well you have managed time.

A. My top long-term career goals are:
1. ______________________________
2. ______________________________
3. ______________________________
4. ______________________________
5. ______________________________

B. The most important of these is: ______________________________

____

C. Five tasks that will most help me attain this most important long-term goal are:
1. ______________________________
2. ______________________________
3. ______________________________
4. ______________________________
5. ______________________________

D. The first task I must complete to achieve it is: ______________________________

____

E. The five most crucial steps for the next six months are:
1. ______________________________
2. ______________________________
3. ______________________________
4. ______________________________
5. ______________________________

F. The single most important step for the next six months is: ______________________________

____

____

G. Five tasks that will help me complete this most important step for the next six months are:

1. ________________________________
2. ________________________________
3. ________________________________
4. ________________________________
5. ________________________________

H. The first task I must complete to reach my most important step is:

____

____

THE NATURAL "BREAKS"

Now that you have salvaged some time for important things, let's put it to the best possible use. As you look at the calendar, there are natural breaks in your work schedule. They may be vacation times, three-day weekends, holidays, a birthday, or other special days. Select three or four of these break times in the next three months, then plan your future schedule to take the greatest possible advantage of these breaks. For each chosen date, set the goal of completing some appropriate assignment or activity. Plan to start something new and challenging on the other side of each break.

Keep the time schedule for the next three months and work to accomplish your goals and to get your new projects started—all on schedule.

Project or Assignment To Be Completed	Chosen Calendar-Break Dates	New Project or Assignment To Be Started

As you look at each day's schedule, you will see that there are natural breaks there, too. If there is a short time between two scheduled blocks of time, what tasks would be appropriate for using the time to greatest benefit? ____________________

____

Which things can be handled when you are waiting for an appointment? ______________________________

____

Which tasks could be handled during travel time? __________

____

Consider these transitional times carefully. Some tasks can be adapted to make use of time that would otherwise be lost.

IS YOUR CONCENTRATION SLIPPING?

Take This Quick Quiz and See

Effectiveness in time management is directly related to the ability to concentrate. Have you found your mind wandering lately:? Are you having trouble focusing on the task at hand? Indicate whether you **Strongly Agree (SA), Agree (A) Disagree (D)** or **Strongly Disagree (SD)** with each of the following statements:

1. I'm usually trying to work on more than two tasks at the same time.
2. I'm easily upset and bothered by arguments at home or work.
3. I work long hours and rarely have time for lunch or even a break.
4. I'm spending less and less time on physical activities, hobbies, and other leisure pursuits.

5. I often work under distracting conditions where noise, people, or lighting impede my accomplishments.
6. I can never get my tasks organized.
7. My job is no longer challenging; I'm bored and lack the motivation to get things done.
8. I often stay up late at night to get my job done.
9. I seem to be more irritable and cranky lately. I'm not as patient with others as I used to be, and I blow up easily.
10. At the end of the day, I feel I am farther behind than when I started.

Now score yourself by giving 10 points to each **SA** answer, 7 to each **A**, 3 to each **D**, and 0 to each **SD**.

If your score is:

0–20	You've got your act together and know how to concentrate.
21–50	You're doing well and are usually in control.
51–85	You're wasting a lot of time on distractions, and your job performance is reduced.
86–100	You enjoy distractions and will have difficulty keeping a good job.

Procrastination gives away any possible advantage.

More Time Management Ideas

Whenever possible, delegate tasks that are routine, yet time-consuming. For example, opening the mail and tagging the important correspondence can usually be handled by an assistant. Computers can prioritize incoming messages. No matter how few employees you have to rely on, you can always delegate a certain number of tasks. Others can easily:

1. Return less important telephone calls.
2. Compose standard memos.
3. Proofread documents.
4. Prepare for meetings.

If delegating to an employee is not an option for you, try handling your mundane tasks in less time-consuming ways:

5. Combine tasks by opening mail while returning phone calls and by placing conference calls.
6. Plan ahead.
7. Just say "no" politely. If your boss asks you to interrupt important work to do a less important task, find a diplomatic way to make him see your priorities your way. (Usually, your priorities support his, so remind him of your mutual priorities. Offer to do the other task later.)

If you have a boss, learn to look at the big picture and decide what's really important for you to do for her. The higher your boss rises in the company, the more she'll be deluged with trivial paperwork. You can free up her energy to do what she's best at by keeping your eye on your targeted professional objectives. Some of these may be:

8. Consistently completing tasks and projects on time.
9. When possible, relaying information through group meetings rather than numerous meetings with individuals.
10. Taking the initiative when you see work that needs to be done or problems that need to be solved. Don't wait for your boss to point them out.

By accomplishing these objectives in a proactive way, you'll not only position yourself favorably with your boss, you'll get a feeling for how she prioritizes her objectives. You might even be able to help her prioritize.

BE FLEXIBLE

Just as prioritizing is essential, it's also important to be flexible when changes occur. When you learn that it's time to switch gears or change directions, you can remain in charge by being flexible. Realize that it's the nature of things to change—especially in corporate America. Be able to accept new schedules, adjust your objectives, and move forward actively. By accepting change you'll demonstrate your professionalism.

Don't allow yourself to lose because you ran out of time.

Savvy employees know that change opens opportunities to move upward in their organization. Whether your company is undergoing a merger or your department is getting new office furniture, show that you're able to deal with delays and uncertainty. Don't rigidly cling to old game plans. Instead, make up new ones. Seize opportunities by being receptive to your boss's new strategies. Even with a boss who frequently changes his mind, don't throw in the towel. Throw your support behind the new game plan, have fun with it, and plan to stick to it—until things change.

SEVEN WAYS TO GET MORE DONE DURING THE NORMAL WORK DAY

When you come right down to it, your productivity is a very personal thing, but increasing it is not usually easy to accomplish. Here are seven practical approaches that can be helpful separately or in combination:

1. **Do it immediately**. Rush jobs do deserve priority, but all work should be weighed for relative importance.

2. **Don't avoid unpleasant tasks**. The problem of avoiding an unpleasant task is that you carry its emotional burden (of neglect) with you, and that slows you down.
3. **Take care of the easier jobs first**. For the slow starter, this can be a good way to get up a head of steam, and, hopefully, the momentum will keep you going. A good list of accomplishments early in the day can provide an emotional uplift to get you through more trying tasks later in the day. There are other situations in which this technique is useful. At a meeting in which controversial decisions must be reached, for example, better relations may result if the easier problems are resolved first.
4. **Do jobs in the order of their importance.** This can be an excellent approach unless all the important jobs are tiring and/or boring. It is not an excuse to put off the items of lesser priority, however, so be sure that *all* tasks are handled within a reasonable period of time.
5. **Alternate difficult tasks with easy tasks.** Alternating the difficult with the easy will give you an occasional rest and gives you something to look forward to. The variety can increase your motivation.
6. **Group similar tasks**. It's just good sense to complete several jobs that require the same data, the same materials, or the same personnel before going on to something else. It reduces duplication of effort and provides momentum as you move from one task to the next. Be sure that you don't use this approach as a means of avoiding other, less appealing tasks, however.
7. **Change tasks abut every two hours**. This approach can be particularly helpful when you are doing routine, monotonous tasks. A different type of work can relieve the

boredom, lift the spirits, and give you something to anticipate.

The Time of Your Life

Time is:

- **A Gift**—It comes to you at birth. Only you can decide what to do with it. It cannot be bought, sold or bartered.
- **A Precious Resource**—Nothing has more value. When time is gone, life is gone.
- **Equally Distributed**—Everyone has the same amount. Whether poor or rich, old or young, man, woman, or child, we all have twenty-four hours each day.
- **Unpredictable**—Only God knows how much total time we have on this earth. The challenge is to make the best possible use of whatever years, months, days, hours, and minutes we have.
- **Disciplinary**—We can choose to abuse our time or use it wisely. There is no middle ground. Remaining neutral has a consequence: Someone else will decide for us.
- **A Responsibility**—Time cannot be delegated or given away. It is ours and only ours. There is no escape from its burden. There is no substitute for its opportunities.
- **A Trust**—Misuse of time betrays a trust. The gift of time and the freedom to use it are the foundations for all opportunity.
- **Easily Abused**—Adults have no excuse for time loss. Ignorance, neglect, blame, and circumstance are all shallow self-deceit.
- **Fleeting**—None of life's events are duplicated *exactly*. Time is not stalked and captured. It is planned, then grasped and used with all available energy and talent.
- **A River**—Time flows by without stopping. It is powerful. It is relentless. It is renewing. It is a source that enables us to transform our abilities into action.

Applying these concepts can change your life if you let them. Will you?

© Copyright Roger Fritz & Associates Inc.

Conclusion

Improvement in time management comes only to those who understand that time is an irreplaceable resource—once used, it is gone forever. Effective people discipline themselves to use the tools in this section wisely and continuously.

Just a Minute

Life is just a minute,
only sixty seconds in it.
Forced upon me, can't refuse it,
didn't seek, didn't choose it,
but it's up to me to use it.
I must suffer if I lose it,
give account if I abuse it.
Just a tiny little minute,.
but eternity is in it.

—Anonymous

Step 6

Are You Confident?

Self-confidence is a basic ingredient of resilience. People who cannot direct themselves—who wait for others to tell them what to do because they lack the confidence to determine their own direction—are very handicapped when it comes to bouncing back. You need to be able to create your own future . . . not your own failure!

I have always felt that self-confidence is incremental. It is built little by little, and the earlier you start building, the better. If, for instance, you can help children gradually improve the skills they are interested in, by the time they are teens they will be prepared to move forward in these areas without constant reassurance or hand-holding.

In adults, self-confidence is strongly linked to the willingness to take risks. Self-confident people don't worry endlessly about what might happen if something fails. They know that if one venture doesn't work out, something else will. And they know that if they do falter, they won't tumble all the way down to the bottom—they'll fall back to that ledge of self-confidence that underpins all their efforts, and start again from there.

TEST YOUR SELF-CONFIDENCE

	Never	Sometimes	Often
■ Do you tend to envy the accomplishments of others close to you?	☐	☐	☐
■ Do you usually think you—rather than someone else—are wrong?	☐	☐	☐
■ Do you think others tend to talk about you behind your back?	☐	☐	☐
■ Do you often wish you were someone else?	☐	☐	☐
■ Have you looked back on a lot of missed opportunities because you didn't try?	☐	☐	☐
■ Do you tend to be afraid of failing?	☐	☐	☐
■ Does criticism bother you?	☐	☐	☐
■ Have you avoided relationships because you might be rejected?	☐	☐	☐
■ Are you concerned that you eat, smoke, or drink too much?	☐	☐	☐
■ Are you embarrassed when you are complimented?	☐	☐	☐
■ Do you tend to make excuses when you lose?	☐	☐	☐
■ Do you think your social skills and appearance are usually inferior?	☐	☐	☐
■ Do you usually compare yourself to others unfavorably?	☐	☐	☐
■ Have you been told that you overcompensate for your uncertainties by being boastful, aggressive, hostile, or withdrawn?	☐	☐	☐
■ Do you usually let others initiate action?	☐	☐	☐

Scoring: If you answered "often" or "sometimes" one to three times, you have a high level of self-confidence; four to seven times indicates a moderate level of confidence and suggests that you may have reason to be concerned; answering "often" or "sometimes" eight or more times suggests that self-doubt is a major factor in your make-up and keeps you from enjoying adequate self-confidence.

> **You may already be a loser.**
> —Sweepstakes letter received by Rodney Dangerfield

CREATE YOUR OWN FUTURE—NOT YOUR OWN FAILURE!

As difficult as it may be to believe, some people actually create failure for themselves. Such situations are setups that feed the individual's insecurity and lack of confidence, and they are a breeding ground for stress.

Learning to recognize and avoid situations that lead to failure will reduce your on-the-job stress. By eliminating such situations, you'll improve your chances for success. Here are some examples of how you may be creating your own failure:

- You habitually accept more work than you possibly can get done.
- You create, and then don't meet, unrealistic personal deadlines.
- You must be number one in everything that you do.
- You acknowledge only what you do wrong and ignore what you do right.
- Without any evidence to that effect, you believe that you have disappointed someone important to you.
- You set, then fail to meet, perfectionist standards.
- You feel cheated and insecure every time someone else gets ahead.
- You have developed the habit of procrastinating.

No matter how hard we try, we all fail at one time or another.

Failure is part of being human. Learn from your failure. Ask yourself how you can avoid a similar failure in the future. When something doesn't work, look at it as a chance to try something new. Devise a new method or plan to replace the failed one. Remember, all successful people learn to overcome failure. It is a necessary stage on the road to success!

> **Winners expect to win.**
> **Life is a self-fulfilling prophecy.**

TRIVIAL PURSUITS FOR AMBITIOUS PEOPLE

Ambition and self-confidence are not the same thing. Too often, ambitious people sidetrack themselves by pursuing what I call **trivial pursuits.**

Those who are most successful have found ways to avoid the temptation of diversions that waste time, energy, and resources. Here are a few of these trivial pursuits, which have enticed a lot of victims, along with the response they are likely to evoke from a boss or employees:

Trivial Pursuit	Likely Response
"My experience will carry me through."	Maybe, but remember—it's a "what-have-you-done-for-me-lately world."
"My work is more important than yours."	Almost guaranteed to encourage strong opposition.
"What I do with my personal time has nothing to do with my work."	Right! Now as your boss, I'll delegate this to someone else, and they'll move to the top of my "promotable" list.

Trivial Pursuit	**Likely Response**
"I'm better qualified than you."	Nurtures a built-in resistance to your ideas.
"If I increase my credentials, I should be better paid."	Performance counts more than credentials.
"Don't make waves."	No waves, no progress.
"Whose fault is this?"	If you want to find someone to blame, you always will. More important is to find out *what* is wrong and start to fix it.
"Give them what they ask for—no more, no less."	Avoiding problems and playing it safe are not the same as success.
"If you knew what I know about this, you would understand my decision better."	I'll *never* know if you won't tell me.
"I didn't have time for that."	Wrong. You didn't *take* time for it.
"*You* have a problem."	Better to say "*We* have a problem" or ask "How can I help you?"
"*They* can't make up their minds."	In management, *they* are *us*.
"If you don't like it, you can quit."	But the problem won't go away.
"I don't care what you think, this is the way it will be."	If you won't let me help you, you don't need me.

LEARN TO SAY NO

It's Difficult, But Someone Has to Do It

Many people find it very difficult to say no. Having to deny someone's request is psychologically unpleasant, whether the individual making the request is a member of the family or an employee on the job.

A supervisor knows that saying no invites the person who has been refused to complain to friends and coworkers that "the boss has been unreasonable (or unfair)."

Popular decisions are not necessarily right.

We also fear that, in some sense, a refusal will disappoint and thereby hurt the petitioner.

Being too blunt when announcing your decision (refusal) may get it over with more quickly from your point of view; but to the disappointed person, bluntness generally seems to indicate an unwillingness to give the proposal a reasonable amount of consideration, a tendency to "shoot from the hip," and perhaps even a feeling that the decision was made on the basis of personality rather than sound business reasoning.

Still, refusals very often *must* be made, and the most painless way to do it involves three steps:

1. Bite the bullet and DO it. Say, "No, I cannot (will not) grant your request."
2. Give the individual a reason or an explanation for your refusal. Knowing the reason may change the perception that you are unreasonable or arbitrary.
3. Show the individual that their needs are important and that you would like to be able to meet them. If possible, offer an alternate course of action or an alternate solution by saying, "I can't meet your request, but I can . . ." This will help the individual understand your reasons for refusal, and you will overcome a feeling of rejection.

And unless you are in an extremely critical situation, try to avoid snap decisions. Tell the individual that you will take the request under consideration and give him or her a decision in a day or two.

Do not procrastinate or wait until the last minute to announce your decision, but do take enough time to give the person the feeling that the request has had a fair hearing.

HOW TO BEAT THE ODDS

Become a bullet-biter.
Select friends carefully.
Be careful whom you learn from.
Listen to those who love you.
Know before you talk.
Don't experiment with values.
Don't curse adversity.
Never substitute excuses for hard work.
Learn where to find what you don't know.
THINK.
Never compromise morals.
Respect only those who earn it.
Make persistence your legacy
Don't delay—perform.

DEVELOP YOUR CONFIDENCE BY IDENTIFYING AND EASING YOUR ANXIETIES AT WORK

Many people—particularly business owners and managers—allow their self-confidence to be eroded by stress and anxiety. Often, people in such a position act as though they don't like it. Why so many complaints? Why so much pressure? Why is anxiety so prevalent among those who should be able to have the greatest influence on their employees?

My answer is that most people in leadership positions aren't deliberate enough about dealing with the inevitable strain in their lives. They think tension will just disappear if they don't dwell on it. Not true!

A realistic approach to anxiety management, it seems to me, involves five stages. You must:

1. Identify the source of your tension.
2. Select the particular burdens you want to deal with.
3. Be realistic about the barriers to overcoming them.
4. Develop a personal stress management program.
5. Make the plan work.

> **A great actor can bring tears to your eyes, but then, so can a bad boss.**

Stage 1: Identifying the Sources of Stress

The following checklist can help identify the sources of your tension. Consider each item carefully, and indicate how much of a strain it is for you on the following scale: 1=never, 2=seldom, 3=sometimes, 4=often, 5=always.

1.	I am unclear about my priorities at work.	______
2.	Others' demands for my time at work can't be satisfied.	______
3.	Health or other personal problems are on my mind almost every day.	______
4.	There are too many demands on me.	______
5.	I fear I am not well qualified for the job I have now.	______
6.	I am concerned about the effectiveness of some of the people I must count on.	______
7.	There is little chance for the company to become what I want it to be.	______
8.	I never seem to have time to finish what I start.	______
9.	I have to work under conditions in which I can't do my best.	______
10.	I have too much to do and too little time to do it.	______

11. I don't have the support I need at home. ______
12. I often can't rely on the loyalty of some key employees. ______
13. The fear of failure is constantly on my mind. ______
14. I have a poor relationship with some of the people I must work with regularly. ______
15. I am interrupted too much. ______
16. I feel pressure from home about my work hours. ______
17. I spend my time fighting fires rather than carrying out a plan. ______
18. My company is continually threatened by financial problems. ______
19. I don't have the opportunity to use my special knowledge and skills in my work. ______
20. It seems I always move from one deadline to another. ______

TOTAL ______________

Scoring Key

A Total of	**Indicates**	**Action Needed**
90-100	Severe anxiety	Change overdue
80-90	Dangerous anxiety	Change now
70-80	Moderate anxiety	Change necessary
60-70	Abnormal anxiety	Change soon
50-60	Normal anxiety	Change selectively
Under 50	Anxiety should not be a factor in your effectiveness	

Stage 2: The Priorities

As you study each item on this checklist, specific reasons for your response will come to mind: names of people, events, circumstances, disappointments, problems, and frustrations. The key to anxiety management lies in your ability to go beyond these negatives.

Rank the stressors on the list in terms of severity. Give an "A" rating to the five stressors that are causing you the most anxiety.

Give a "B" rating to the five stressors that are next in the level of anxiety they cause you. Give a "C" rating to the next five stressors. Give a "D" rating to the five stressors that are causing you the least amount of stress right now.

Stage 3: The Barriers

Now you are ready to think through the barriers to progress. Suppose you put time pressures (such those listed in items 2, 4, 8, 10, 15, 16, 17 and 20) in your "A" group. Answer the following questions about each item:

- Why is this important?
- What are the causes?
- Can I solve it alone?
- If not, who can help me?
- What must I do first?
- When will I begin?
- How will I monitor progress?

Stage 4: The Plan of Action

Now you have the beginning of a Personal Anxiety Management Plan. While there are no techniques that are guaranteed to alleviate tension, a number of practical, commonsense guidelines can help you bring it under control:

- **Ventilate** the problem to a confidant. This tends to broaden perspectives and unclutter the mind, making it possible to arrive at a sensible course of action. Select someone you can trust, who is not only an excellent listener but who will keep your confidence.
- **Find someone worse off.** Not every situation is a life or death proposition. Don't worry about the little things. Visit a nursing home to see firsthand how small your problems

really are. You will not only live longer, but you will solve more problems faster and with better results.

If you can dream it, you can do it.—Walt Disney

- **Focus on positive consequences.** Convince yourself that you can make use of the stressful event in your personal development. For example, "Now I realize that I must never get myself in this kind of a situation with my boss again." This will not only help you grow, but it will reduce the after-effects of the tension. As the old saying goes, anything that doesn't kill you makes you stronger.
- **Don't wait too long.** If the anxiety is strong enough to bother you, do something. Chances are that waiting won't make it any better. In fact, delays on your part are likely to increase the pain.
- **Take charge.** Put yourself in a position to either divert or stop whatever is increasing the anxiety. If you must make an important presentation, prepare for it. If you have something to get off your chest, do it soon. You will probably feel less stressed after doing so.
- **Congratulate yourself.** When you've been eyeball to eyeball with a difficult event and faced it down, give yourself credit. Not only has your skill brought the difficulty under control, but you can now take on other problems with more confidence. This new assurance will help you cope more effectively with new problems as they arise and will enable you to make the most of them.

Many people can bounce back from strain without too much difficulty. They survive and succeed because of their overall positive attitude. No matter how bleak things look, these people maintain an optimistic inner spirit that helps them surmount obstacles. They refuse to acknowledge defeat—to them, defeats are merely temporary setbacks.

Stage 5: Making Your Plan Work

To deal with each stressor adequately, you should evaluate its frequency, severity, and net effect. To put your analysis in focus, you should record and track your commitments to action.

When anxiety caused by any one particular situation has been eliminated or brought under control, take on the other stressors you have identified in order of their priority.

Both slow and fast runners can stumble.

By and large, tension results from facing the unknown consequences of change. Change is inevitable, so anxiety is inevitable. Tension ebbs and flows in direct relationship to your overall sense of adequacy.

Above all, remember that coping with anxiety is a personal matter. Only *you* can do it for yourself.

Stressful circumstances reveal the true nature of your leadership. Little by little, you grow either stronger or weaker, until one day a crisis reveals what you have already become.

If you plan to be promotable, you can never totally eradicate difficult situations. But you can find ways to minimize their impact. In so doing, you will accomplish two vital objectives: (1) you will maintain your competitive edge, and (2) you will prove to the executives who make selections that you are qualified to absorb responsibilities for leadership beyond what you can accomplish by yourself.

Think about it: What can you do today to minimize the effects of nonproductive tension?

To bounce back from defeat and setbacks, you must be an accountable person who accepts responsibility for yourself and for your actions.

ACCOUNTABILITY AND SELF-CONFIDENCE

Accountability is a precious asset in a free society. It does not happen by accident. It is not directly related to credentials, or education, or expertise, or even experience. What we call twenty years of experience may, in reality, be one year of experience and nineteen years of repetition.

If you consistently try to find someone to blame when things go wrong, you'll succeed 100 percent of the time. But to improve things—and to improve yourself—you need to focus on *what's* wrong, not *who* is wrong. Blame others, and the people who work with or for you will do as little as possible, playing it safe while they wait for someone else to step forward. Therefore, if you tend to be a blame-thrower, stop and think about what you are doing. You are discouraging the people you need most—the people who are your best producers.

Accountability precedes improvement. The never-ending quest for all leaders at all times and in all places is to answer the question, "What do we mean by performance here?"

Performance requires accountable people, and accountable people always determine *who* will do *what* by *when*. This principle is frequently overlooked in the rush toward employee empowerment. Empowered people who are not accountable spin their wheels.

THANK GOD THE HOLE IS IN YOUR SIDE OF THE BOAT!

How many people do you know who have the outlook that everything bad that happens is someone else's fault—that blame always belongs elsewhere—that they should always be immune from criticism? These are the people—naïve at best and dangerous at worst—who don't see the implications of their involvement, even when the boat is sinking!

How do such people stray so far from reality? Usually, poor role models and/or excessive ego are to blame. What can be done about it. Answering the following ten questions may reveal whether you are avoiding accountability or permitting others to do so. Score each question on a scale of 0 (lousy) to 10 (excellent). Be honest.

Informative—Do I give other people information *before* they need it?	______
Realistic—Do I set priorities, negotiate goals, and monitor progress?	______
Teacher—Do I help people learn from their mistakes?	______
Analytical—Am I more interested in facts than opinions, but open to recommendations?	______
Predictable—Can people anticipate my actions and reactions reliably, or am I inclined to change my mind without notice?	______
Clearly competitive—Do I share credit? Am I more concerned about what's wrong than about who's wrong?	______
Firm but fair—Am I influenced more by political factors or by social ties than by performance?	______
Restrained—Do I jump to conclusions?	______
Modest—Do I lose gracefully and win without gloating?	______
Amicable—Do I keep old grudges or penalize past mistakes?	______
TOTAL	______

If your score is:

70 or above	You're pitching in to plug the holes.
From 50–70	You're hoping someone else will plug them.

If your score is:

From 30–50	You're likely to have the people who didn't plug the holes thrown overboard.
Under 30	You're going to sink and never know why.

Why Responsibility Is Avoided

Despite the many advantages of taking on new responsibilities, we aren't always eager to do so. Why? Here are some possible reasons:

1. **Lack of decision-making power**. The boss always has the final word on every subject. No need to waste effort thinking through ways to do a difficult job, only to have them rejected.
2. **Fear of criticism** for mistakes. Negative or unreasonable criticism can lead to reluctance to take on responsibility.
3. **Lack of necessary resources** and facts. Little will be taken on if every step is a struggle.
4. **Burden shifting.** It is easier to shift the burden and ask the boss to decide. This becomes a habit, but employees can break it.
5. **Inadequate incentives**—failure to give credit and rewards.
6. **Lack of self-confidence**. Lots of guidance and support is needed to offset this problem.
7. **Too much work**. Additional assignments won't be appealing if employees are already overloaded.
8. **Anxiety about ability** to do the job well. Training may be the solution.
9. **Inability to see the value of the assignment** in relation to unit and organizational objectives.

Sometimes teamwork is a process used to determine which people will be getting the blame.

The Confidence Circle

I believe that self-confidence grows every time you achieve a goal, overcome an obstacle, or face down a fear. This illustration shows the continuum between confidence and achievement:

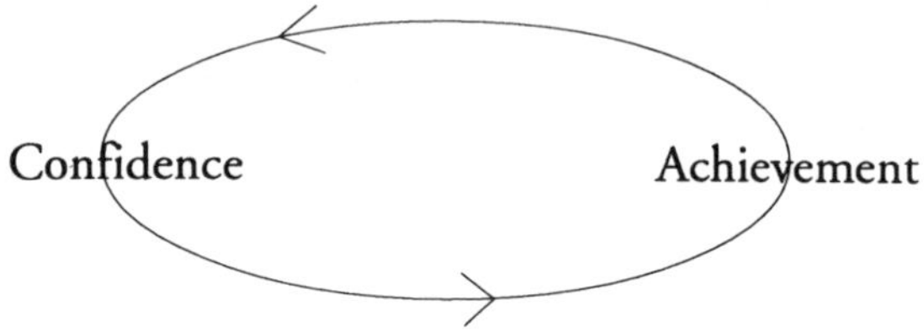

When you succeed in one area, you are primed to succeed in another. Your successes feed on one another, so let them dine often!

> **Being powerful is like being a lady. If you have to tell people you are, you aren't** — Margaret Thatcher

SELF-CONFIDENCE AND POWER

Many people mistake arrogance for self-confidence. Truly self-confident people are modest, not loud; they may remain in the background instead of thrusting themselves into the limelight. In fact, I've often found that the loudest and most obnoxious people are not at all self-confident. Their noisiness is a thin veneer stretched over a bundle of anxieties and fears. While many self-confident people are powerful, power does not necessarily lead to confidence. Many people in positions of power are very insecure.

Step 7

Who Needs You?

My one-line prescription for success in the workplace is this: Make yourself needed! If you can do that, you will be employable *and* you will stand out wherever you go.

Leaders *always* need help.

The legend of Robin Hood endures not to amplify the oft-repeated theme "Take from the rich and give to the poor"—that's a territory already claimed by the federal government. No, Robin Hood is remembered because he succeeded in making himself needed! What lessons can we learn from him?

- **Don't wait for someone else to fight your battles;** take initiative yourself. Everyone cursed the evil sheriff, but no one resisted him until Robin showed them how.
- **Don't curse those who have more than you do**. Work so you can have what you want. Every person with a skill to offer was welcome, from cook, to hunter, to woodsman, to bowman.
- **Don't trust conventional ways to succeed**. Improvise.

Robin's band used their forest home as an advantage in surprising their enemies.

- **Don't put all of your confidence in like-minded people;** find strength in diversity. Little John was known as an outcast until he joined Robin's band.

Jealousy destroys.

- **Don't assume you will get what you want by waiting**. The prize usually goes to those who take the first step. Time after time, the Merrymen defeated the sheriff with the element of surprise.
- **Don't limit your intentions to words only**. Show what must be done, take action, and lead. Robin himself was a good bowman and was always at the forefront in battle.
- **Don't put your confidence in credentials alone**. Friar Tuck was more than a priest.
- **Don't let jealousy or resentment cloud your judgment**. Petty people don't produce. Robin didn't resent Little John's superior strength—he welcomed it, praised it, and used it.
- **Don't allow regrets about the past to dominate your life today**. If this happens, you will become your own worst enemy. Maid Marian's hand in marriage was a sidebar. The real goal was freedom from oppression.

Robin Hood remains a hero because his personal instincts and judgments were rooted in the three words that are a timeless link between leadership and service: **Make yourself needed!**

WHAT DO YOU OFFER?

Before you can determine how to make yourself needed, you need to find out what you can offer. Self-analysis and self-appraisal are

It's not the most intellectual job in the world, but I do have to know the letters. — *Wheel of Fortune's Vanna White*

essential tools for anyone trying to bounce back from defeat or trying to get ahead. Successful professionals evaluate themselves before others do. They never wait to be fired!

Having an objective understanding of who you are allows you to accept the parts you like and work on changing those you don't. It also helps you clarify what you offer your employer, customers, or employees, and makes it easier to separate constructive feedback from unwarranted criticism.

These four elements are essential to self-evaluation:

1. Understanding your work habits.
2. Understanding your strengths and weaknesses.
3. Setting up goals for improvement.
4. Monitoring your progress.

If you are not willing to start with yourself, forget about making yourself needed. It's not likely to happen. And if it does, it won't last long.

What Are Your Work Habits?

Maybe you have just started in a new position, or perhaps you've been at your job so long you could do your work in your sleep. Has the grind gotten to you, or do you look at each day's challenges as uniquely different? You can find out where you stand by answering the following questions:

- Am I dependable?
- Do I take pride in my work?

- Do I steer clear of destructive office politics?
- Do I try to learn from my mistakes?
- Do I approach problems as an opportunity to learn new skills?

Dependability means being at work on time, sometimes arriving early and staying late, meeting deadlines, keeping your promises. Your behavior sets an example to those both below and above you on the corporate ladder. Even a somewhat lazy and disorganized boss will improve his performance when he knows he has conscientious, talented employees on his team who are prepared for meetings.

Pride in your work sends another clear message. Working by the project, not by the clock, means that, if necessary, you're willing to dedicate time after work and on weekends to see that a project is done right and deadlines are met. No matter how long you've been in the same position, sloppiness and laziness are not acceptable.

To give your sense of dedication a boost:

- Find new approaches to doing your job.
- Ask for training on new technology.
- Job-share your present position with someone else in the company.
- Attend a motivational seminar.
- Find out how people in similar positions innovate in their jobs. Do this in other companies as well as your own.
- Explore the possibility of using your knowledge and experience to train for a new job within the company.

Above all, *steer clear of harmful office politics—spreading* malicious gossip and rumors. When you're in a managerial position, office rumors can be an important way of obtaining information you may otherwise be denied. But it's crucial to keep a professional attitude and to be supportive of fellow workers—especially your boss.

To monitor your work habits and make sure you are working at peak productivity, devise a checklist that ranks all of your job duties in order of importance. Revise it weekly to make sure you are touching all of your bases but focusing primarily on your most important tasks.

What Are Your Assets and Liabilities?

Take an hour or so to reflect on your activities in the last year. Ask yourself, "What were my major achievements (results) in the past year, and how were they related to my objectives?"

Objectives

What goals did you and your boss agree that you were to accomplish in the last year?

Achievements

How did you do in meeting your objectives? If you didn't meet them, why not? Did your boss have advance warning that your goals would not be met? Were you in control of the reasons why you didn't meet them? If not, why not?

Perhaps you underestimated the costs required to increase sales or production and did not make your case strong enough before budgets were approved. Or, perhaps you were ordered to make these improvements, believing all along that they were impossible, but never saying so. When that happens, you must take some of the blame.

For more insights into your assets and liabilities, answer the following questions:

- What major dissatisfactions do you have with your performance during the past year? Does your boss agree?

- What are your most important assets in performing the job you now hold? Does your boss agree?
- On a scale of 1–100, rate your chances of being selected for your present job if you were to reapply in open competition.
- Would you want to reapply? If not, why?
- What are the areas of personal development in which you most need to improve?
- What have you learned during the past year that will help you in your work in the future? Does your boss agree?
- Other than your present assignment, what would you be well qualified to do in your company? Do you know what you must do to qualify?

If you think you are indispensable, do two things: (1) Visit a nursing home, and (2) Attend a funeral.

What Are Your Goals?

The best companies have mission statements; so should you. Take time to write down both long- and short-term goals. Start with the long-term goals because they will determine your short-term goals. Be as creative as you like. Don't limit yourself by defining goals that can only be achieved in your present job. Long-term goals can relate to work, family, hobbies, and recreations—any part of your life you truly want to develop. Your list could look something like this:

1. Be a better parent; spend more time with my children.
2. Finish documentation project for new computer system at work.
3. Improve my tennis game.
4. Research family history.

5. Improve communication with my boss. Seek clarification of her expectations and identify a method of evaluation.
6. Write a romance novel.
7. Identify ways to become more innovative and demonstrate leadership at work.
8. Become my company's first female vice president.

Now prioritize the list. As much fun as writing a romance novel would be, chances are it's going to be outranked by finishing the documentation project at work. Yet spending more time with your children and spouse is clearly an important consideration. Managing your time better and constantly re-prioritizing and delegating small tasks could free up some time and energy to spend with the family.

Those who have family models to follow are the richest heirs.

Look for the fundamental issues: your commitment to your family, the need for advancement and recognition at work, a desire to take on a creative project, and so on. It is important that you understand what issues are basic to your life and their priority. This understanding will help you resolve conflicts with yourself, at home, and at work.

For instance, you are offered a promotion at work, but the new job requires a significant amount of travel. This means you would spend much less time with your spouse and children. What do you do? Do you accept or decline the job? The answer depends on the way you've structured your priorities. Here is a series of questions you can ask yourself to help resolve family/career conflicts:

- What are my career goals?

- How have they changed in the past few years?
- What are my goals for my family?
- How have they changed in the past few years?
- Do my actions interfere with my progress toward realizing these goals?
- What elements in my life are in conflict with my career goals?
- Is the position I currently hold really the best one for me?
- Am I afraid of failing to meet my goals?
- Am I afraid of meeting my goals?
- Am I prepared to adjust my career ambition?

These questions may prove difficult to answer, but you will feel more comfortable with your decision if you've clearly defined and prioritized the fundamental issues in your life.

Short-term goals are the stepping stones whereby you reach long-term goals. To achieve better communication with your boss and associates, you could set up monthly short-term communication goals. For example:

- Establish a method for passing on information to my boss.
- Make sure my boss is passing on vital information to me that she has received from upper management. If necessary, remind her that good communication allows both of us to do our jobs better.
- When appropriate, schedule weekly meetings between staff and management to keep projects on schedule.
- Solicit feedback from staff regarding the effectiveness of meetings. Ask for ways to help make their jobs easier. Is there training or technical information they need? Are the meetings helpful?

Are You Monitoring Your Progress?

To make sure the goals you set are accomplished, not forgotten, ask yourself the following questions every six months:

- How well have I performed in my overall goals?
- Were they worth achieving?
- Were they worth achieving for my company?
- Based on these answers, what new goals would produce gain for me and for my company?

Assessing your own performance in the workplace can help you pinpoint strengths you can develop and weaknesses you need to overcome. A solid sense of your abilities, coupled with clear goals, can help you focus on how you can make yourself needed—and what you hope to get out of it.

You may think this is all too formal. You may not want to take the time to do it. You may prefer to simply wait and see what happens. After all, you're not in serious trouble. Things are going fine. There is no reason to believe that your chances for advancement aren't equal to everyone else's. Why worry? Why act as if bad things are bound to happen if you don't act now?

Look around. How many truly successful people do you know who got there and stayed there without hard work and serious self-examination? Even heirs to great family fortunes have no guarantee of survival.

The Wrong Credentials for the Job

A Chicago bank once asked a Boston investment firm for a letter of recommendation for a young Bostonian they were considering hiring. The investment firm could not say enough about the young man. His father, they wrote, was a Cabot, his mother was a Lowell, and farther back, he was a blend of Saltonstalls, Peabodys, and others of Boston's oldest families. In other words, he was highly recommended. Several days later, the Chicago bank replied, "Thanks for your trouble; however, he is not exactly the type we are looking for. We are not," their letter declared, "contemplating using the young man for breeding purposes!"

MORE WAYS TO MAKE YOURSELF NEEDED

Here are ten powerful clues to help make yourself needed now and for the long term:

1. **Go above and beyond expectations.** Help your boss make it easy to decide in your favor to give you the biggest possible raise.
2. **Bring solutions, not problems.** Never blame someone else for your errors. When you do, things always get worse.
3. **Bounce back from mistakes.** Consider them knowledge gained, not discouraging pains.

Failure and success have the same root . . . trying.

4. **Avoid the temptation to make excuses.** Who really cares about your problems? The only real issue is—Are you accountable, or aren't you?
5. **Don't depend on reminders to complete your work.** Set interim deadlines for tasks and meet them.
6. **Shoot for a good record, not perfection.** Accept the reality of some failure and learn from it.

You may have to fight a battle more than once to win it.—Margaret Thatcher

7. **Think ahead—eliminate unpleasant surprises.** The best way to attract favorable attention to yourself *and your boss.*
8. **Don't dwell on successes.** Move on quickly to new projects before compliments become shackles.
9. **Never assume his/her goals are the same as yours without**

negotiating them. Write them down. Meet regularly. Make each day count toward meeting them.

10. **When an agreement is reached, get going!** Those who wait to be told what to do continue to be told what to do. Their value decreases.

RULES FOR RENEWAL:
Twenty Reliable Ways to Put You in Demand and Keep You There

- Don't try to force an event, action, or result whose time has not come. First discover why there is resistance, then overcome the reasons one by one until your solution is obvious.
- Don't trust people whose integrity is unproven. Think of your career as your lifeblood. Would you ever risk accepting a transfusion from a donor who had not been tested for AIDS?
- Believe in results, not activities. Busyness is irrelevant. Only performance counts.

The older generation thought nothing of getting up at 5:00 every morning. The younger generation doesn't think much of it either.

- Follow only those who deserve your loyalty. If uncertain, wait for evidence.
- Beware of those who are committed only to themselves.
    - They will consistently favor their own preferences.
    - They will follow only their own schedule.
    - They will ignore team goals.
    - They will disappear in an emergency.

- Start your own engine and keep it running. If you let someone else keep your ignition key, you'll never even be in the race.
- Don't try to please everyone. Focus on (1) keeping commitments to those you love and (2) the requirements of your work.
- Pace your expenditure of energy. Excessive effort spent on low priorities depletes the amount of energy left for essential duties.
- Don't abuse your body or poison your mind. No one will ever know how many home runs Babe Ruth and Mickey Mantle would have hit if they had taken better care of themselves.
- Avoid negative thinkers. Focus on brainstorming possibilities. Your time is too precious to be wasted imagining catastrophes.
- Shun change resisters. They will soon convince you to join them.
- Disarm with kindness. Nothing frustrates an opponent more than a gift, a favor, or a compliment. It ruins their belief that you are not worthy of respect.
- Live beneath your means. Only if you accumulate a serious reserve will you have the peace of mind that comes from knowing you can handle an unexpected or emergency expense.
- Become an expert in something. Your earning capacity will be directly related to the variety of your expertise and your conscientiousness in using it. Ignore the "wisdom" of basketball star Shaquille O'Neal, who, after signing a seven year, 121 million-dollar contract with the Los Angeles Lakers, said: "I'm tired of hearing about money, money, money. I just want to play the game, drink Pepsi and wear Reebok."

- Face up to your weaknesses. Acknowledge them, but don't let them prevail over your strengths. Only when you capitalize on your strengths will you achieve near your potential. Pro golfer John Daly had this to say about his lack of interest in world literature as a college student: "I couldn't care less about those fiction stories about what happened in the year 1500 or 1600. Half of them aren't even true."
- Take only affordable risks. Don't sit at the poker table if the stakes are too high.
- Don't perpetuate dependence.
  - Financial dependence erases needed skills.
  - Emotional dependence erodes necessary self-esteem.
- Learn to live with little praise. Those who seek to impress with their self-proclaimed wisdom via credentials, experience, travel, or influential friends and relatives, are not only insecure, they are usually inept as well.
- Simplify. Attempts to make life more complicated than it needs to be are not only stressful, they are self-defeating.

Trust yourself. Resist the temptation to waste time, effort, and money trying to become someone you aren't. Then—and only then—will you be ready to lead.

ARE YOU READY FOR PROMOTION?

You are approaching the time when you should be considered for a significant promotion if you can:

- **Survive under a boss who doesn't like you.** The odds of always having a friendly boss are almost nil. Count on it! If you let a bad boss determine your success, you have only yourself to blame.
- **Calm down a belligerent employee.** The best leaders can keep cool in a crisis. If you have shown that you can be a

calming influence on others, you will attract the attention of those who realize the importance of this quality.

- **Handle an incident of sexual harassment.** Situations with sexual overtones are inevitable wherever men and women work together. The two key questions for promotable people are: (1) Have I ever been guilty myself? and (2) Do I know what to do if it happens to me?
- **Deal with being offered a bribe.** Allowing oneself to be susceptible to anything "under the table" is the kiss of death. Reject the offer immediately, and inform your supervisor of your action.
- **Dodge being ripped off by a shady vendor.** Always do your homework. Check records—even those of long-term suppliers. If you can be fooled once, you are a likely to be fooled again, and no boss wants to be embarrassed by a naïve staff member's action.
- **Fill in for an absent speaker.** Make no mistake about it, those who can express themselves well in public will always attract more attention than those who can't. Practice expressing your views in areas where you have experience and expertise.
- **Avoid making fewer concessions than a competitor in a tough negotiation.** You must prove that you know how to avoid giving too much. Anyone can say yes or make concessions that take away all benefit or profit from a deal.
- **Improvise another back-up plan when your original back-up plan fails.** It's not enough to have a "Plan B." Those who are most promotable have thought about third and fourth alternatives. They always challenge themselves to find something that will work.
- **Explain just what it is you do.** If your understanding of what you do and why is vague, you are not a good candidate

to lead others in evaluating their priorities, setting objectives, and negotiating workable action plans.

Try not to become a man of success, but rather a man of value.—Albert Einstein

THINKING: THE UNUSED GIFT

No doubt about it, the greatest gift of all is good health. Without it, life is at best misery and at worst painful death. But, if we are healthy, our next greatest asset is the capability to think.

Unfortunately, God gives us the *ability* to think, but does not guarantee it. Too many Americans are forgetting that basic truth. Here is a good example from today's sports page:

> A rookie football player is competing to be kept on the roster of an NFL team. The final cut is tomorrow. "It's hard," he says, "because you want to just go out and react and play your game without necessarily having to think 'What do I have to do on this play and that play?' You just want to be able to do what comes naturally and show the coaches what kind of talent you have."

News flash: Your talent is useless, young man, if you refuse to think about how to use it!

The greatest gift is to learn to think for yourself.

God enabled us to think so we can reason, judge, discern, analyze, discriminate, evaluate, sift, sort, articulate, decide, reconsider, and then act. But when did you last show your gratitude for this wondrous gift? In what way? A thankful prayer, perhaps? An anonymous gift? A sudden act of kindness?

How about showing your appreciation by becoming a better thinker! What better way to improve yourself and everyone around you. Why? There are some very practical reasons. Thinking is:

- Your best protection against quacks, liars, and cheaters.
- Your best route to advancement.
- Your resistance to bad emotional decisions.
- Your removal of the blinders of prejudice.
- Your means to overcome inertia.
- Your most reliable protection from manipulators.
- Your insurance against unexpected loss.
- Your antidote for those whose charm is really venom.
- Your best bet to avoid fraud and deception.
- Your restorative power to cope with tragedy.
- Your release from the shackles of learned hate.
- Your shield against charismatic, but selfish, "leaders" who only want your vote.
- Your nourishment for recovery.
- Your restraint from repeating mistakes.
- Your defense against deceptive advertising.
- Your strategy to disarm those who would delude you.
- Your armor to break the arrows of those committed to cause you to fail.
- Your resistance of those who would entice you with flattery.
- Your screen for suspicious influences.
- Your tools to unlock unrealized potential.
- Your storehouse providing sustenance for hard times.
- Your stimulant to stop bad habits.
- Your discipline to build on successes.
- Your fortress of defense from unexpected attack.

- Your source for renewal.

Not using your ability to think is the quickest route to failure. Used fully, it offers the most reliable pathway to success. But beware! Thinking is the hardest work there is. It comes easy for no one. Surely, that's why we all avoid it.

Anyone who keeps learning stays young.—Henry Ford

WHAT GOOD IS EXPERIENCE?

Is experience is the best teacher? Sometimes it is, and sometimes it isn't. It all depends on you. Too often, what we call "experience" is nothing but repetition. To be more valuable, we must not only *learn* from experience, we must *apply* what we learn from it and improve upon it.

Experience can be good if:

- It has prepared you for today.
  Looking backward is appropriate only for historians.
- You are comfortable with change.
  Those who resist change get nowhere.
- You welcome new ideas.
  If you don't have new ideas, the other guy wins.
- You scan the horizon for competitive advantage.
  No one else can make you more competitive.
- You never stop exploring.
  Avoiding failure is not the same as success.
- You change wrongs before they become habits.
  The adage "Nothing ventured—nothing gained" is more accurate now than ever.
- You learn to simplify, not complicate.
  Those who try to impress with complicated solutions often want to see others fail.

- You can apply it to current problems.
  Knowledge alone is useless. To make a difference, it must be applied.
- You are committed to renewal.
  Resistance to change is a career killer.
- You use it to stretch to new heights.
  There is no growth while you are protecting yourself from criticism.

Good experiences are building blocks that enable you to create your own future. People who learn to define good experience have laid the foundation for becoming leaders. They are rarely victims. They set the pace.

Gaining *good* experience requires initiative. You can't wait for someone else to provide it. You must risk making mistakes. You must challenge old ways. You must not be afraid of criticism.

Those who make steady (versus sensational) progress are disciplined. They don't think in terms of miracles or even unexpected breakthroughs. They plug away, constantly alert for ways to use what they have learned to move on to the next step.

Experience can be bad if:

- Your skills are out of date.
  - Who is to blame when a low-skilled person is laid off or replaced—the individual or the employer?
- You are locked into old habits.
  - It is always dangerous to be more concerned about appearance than substance.
- You resist change.
  - Don't let yourself be concerned by what hasn't worked before.
  - If you don't believe that change is inevitable, you've been in a deep coma
- You keep reliving the good old days.

- Those who are constantly alert for bad news usually find it.
- You fear making mistakes.
    - Remember, to avoid failure is to limit accomplishment.
- You apply old solutions to new problems.
    - Nothing surpasses the disillusionment of a person whose "tried and true, time-tested" method fails.
- You waste energy on regrets.
    - Doom and gloom is infectious. Don't spread the disease.
- You seek comfort in repetition.
    - The same old ways simply are not good enough in a society where the pace is set by rapidly changing technology.
- You dwell too long on past accomplishments.

  Don't talk about the labor pains, just show me the baby!
- You have followed the wrong people.
    - When you paddle your own canoe, you can do the steering.

Sure, you can learn from bad experiences. But why create them? Why even allow them to happen if they can be prevented?

Bad experiences should not be glossed over. They must be faced and dealt with. If you choose to blame someone else for your bad experiences, you can . . . but you will be the ultimate loser.

To check up on the quality of your current experiences, ask yourself the following questions:

- What are the long-term consequences of this?
- If I continue on this path, will I be better or worse off?
- What am I learning?

Unless you are truly happy as a specialist, consider broadening your career options by adding new skills that will keep you in demand.

Whether you are comfortable with it or not, the best advice that can be given to young people is "Never forget, it's a what-have-you-done-for-me-lately world!"

The keys to minimizing the impact of bad experiences and maximizing benefit from the good experiences are awareness and initiative. Awareness of the above clues will put you on the right track. Taking the initiative to practice the good and eliminate the bad will keep you moving ahead.

Choose a job you love, and you will never have to work a day in your life.—Confucius

CREATIVE PROBLEM-SOLVING

In the War of 1812, the American general William Winder, despite having a four-to-one troop superiority over the British, led his army to defeat and was taken prisoner. The British, however, realized that Winder's incompetence made him an ideal opponent, and they returned him to the American army. Their trust in General Winder was well founded. The British attacked our nation's capitol and burned much of it to the ground, all while Winder was in charge of defending it. That's what you call creative problem-solving.

I return to my original question: Who needs you?

Step 8

Who Will Help You?

Scheduled to speak in Philadelphia at the Town Hall, Bishop Fulton J. Sheen decided to walk from his hotel even though he was unfamiliar with the city. Sure enough, he became lost and was forced to ask some boys to direct him to his destination.

One of them asked Sheen, "What are you going to do there?"

"I'm going to give a lecture," replied the Bishop.

"About what?"

"On how to get to heaven. Would you care to come along?"

"Are you kidding?" said the boy, "You don't even know how to get to Town Hall!"

What is the moral of this little tale? Learn to welcome advice, but choose your advisors carefully! Most of us are not nearly selfish enough about who we can learn from. We just let things happen to us. We let money, geography, our family situation determine where and whom we work for instead of being selective about what we do and where we learn.

Instead, we need to choose our bosses carefully. We deserve to learn from the right people! Likewise, when we become business owners or managers, we need to serve as mentors to our employees.

Learning from a supervisor means looking upward in an

organization. When you're in management, you also need to focus on delegation and motivation. If, as a manager, you have suffered a setback, then as a manager you must overcome it.

Successful people are always aware that they are not "islands." They appreciate the people behind the scenes who helped them.

When you are bouncing back from a reversal, you *can* turn to your boss, your spouse, your coworkers, your employees, and even your customers, for help.

People are happy to lend a hand—*if* they believe you are worthy.

IS YOUR BOSS A WORTHY MENTOR?

There is no doubt that loyalty is never automatic. It must be earned. But how do we decide who deserves our loyalty? My experience has taught me that the boss who deserves loyalty—and can help you as a mentor—fulfills the following requirements:

1. **Worthy bosses prepare well for their position**. Managing is a separate profession or career. People who want to take on a leadership position need to prepare well and continue to grow in office. Good leaders are not born; they are made.
2. **Worthy bosses rate themselves and others *objectively***. Leaders who are subjective about themselves will be subjective in their evaluations of other people. Leaders must be objective in their evaluations and decisions. They must know themselves well.
3. **Worthy bosses initiate change**. Organizations can get hardening of the arteries. Wise leaders know the importance of changing before you have to. They also pay close attention to hiring people who do not resist change.
4. **Worthy bosses work from the inside out**. The most meaningful change begins inside. If your boss says he or she believes in promotion from within, they must devote

time and money to helping people develop. They have to plan ahead for who they are going to have in key leadership positions and they need to know why.

5. **Worthy bosses manage expectations**. Effective leaders clarify expectations regularly. They don't just have a plan, put it in a drawer, and hope it works. They have a way of linking expectations with delivery.
6. **Worthy bosses are good teachers**. Good teachers are good role models—they practice what they teach. Inconsistency kills initiative. People who are good teachers are accessible. They do not depend upon edicts, memos, E-mail, or even voice mail. They are constantly engaged in a process of cutting, fitting, sifting, and sorting to arrive at the best solutions. They create well-informed teams at all levels. They concentrate on preventing problems. They praise and acknowledge the behind-the-scenes people who are usually taken for granted. They weed out those who aren't carrying their load.
7. **Worthy bosses recognize real value**. They quickly discover who gets the best results. They determine who can accept constructive criticism. They realize if you bring people along too fast, they never learn to handle opposition and criticism.
8. **Worthy bosses are management incubators**. They identify and nurture future leaders and reward those who assist them in doing so.
9. **Worthy bosses provide opportunity for personal growth**. They are not afraid of having strong, even aggressive, people reporting to them. They realize that every important project or goal needs a champion—not a committee, but an individual. Leaders must think carefully about what they champion and how critical that project is.
10. **Worthy bosses reward accomplishment, not mediocrity**.

People should be able to feel that their success is directly related to the success of their leaders. Leaders must not only be *willing* to share credit—they must actually do it! They must show by their actions how much they want their team members to succeed.

How does your boss rate? If you're the boss, how do *you* rate? Are you worthy of serving as someone else's mentor?

> **Better a hundred enemies outside the family than one inside.**—*Arabian Proverb*

How Your Spouse Can Help

Your spouse can be an excellent source of help—providing he or she really understands what your job involves and how you feel about it. One of the major, but frequently unnoticed, causes of marital problems, job stress, and career dissatisfaction is that very few people really understand what their spouse does at work. Unless you are a professional athlete whose mistakes are seen on television by millions, a national politician, a highly visible corporate executive, or you are part of a spouse team in a family enterprise, chances are your problems and successes at work are neither understood by, nor shared with, your spouse. I use the word "share," not in the sense of talking about frustrations or complaining about certain people or circumstances, but in terms of in-depth and continuous discussion of what is happening at work, how it is happening, and why.

Three Steps Needed

- The first step is open and continuing discussion. This implies a definition of love that includes a never-ending curiosity about whatever is affecting the work life of one's marriage partner.

- The second step is satisfying that curiosity by regular, firsthand knowledge of their work. How many wives or husbands do you know who regularly visit their spouse's workplace to:
  - See what they do
  - Meet their boss and associates
  - Observe problems
  - Take satisfaction in successes
- The third step is to avoid locking out your mate because you think he or she won't understand or doesn't have adequate background or experience to appreciate your situation. Background and experience are not necessary when the subject is your career. The only vital ingredients are a willingness to listen, to observe, to ask questions, and to empathize. If you do these things, you will be amazed at how little time it takes to become quite knowledgeable in your spouse's field. Not an expert, mind you, but smart enough to be helpful, and that's all that is needed.

TRUST: THE PREREQUISITE FOR GETTING HELP FROM EMPLOYEES

As a manager, your fate is intertwined with that of your people. Success for one and not the other is a certain formula for failure.

To have any chance of long-term success, you must *earn* the respect of those you supervise. To meet this challenge, you must

> **Ignoring the views of those closest to the work is like fertilizing dandelions.**

- Generate a sense of trust by being trustworthy.
- Take the time to understand the needs and expectations of those you supervise.
- Be a good personal example of efficiency and effectiveness.
- Assess the strengths of the people on board, so that their weaknesses will not predominate.

Trust is never achieved easily, particularly when one has the authority to judge the work and worth of others. To create an atmosphere of trust requires you to develop:

- A strong communication network between yourself and those you manage.
- A willingness to support the ideas and efforts of others.
- Predictability in assessments and judgments.
- A sense of fairness and *demonstrated* competence.

Cultivating a sense of trust pays off in many ways:

- Barriers to communication are broken.
- New or pertinent information is identified.
- There's an increased willingness to face problems head-on.

But perhaps the greatest test in cultivating trust can be found in the question almost every employee asks at one time or another: "Does he practice what he preaches?"

Developing the resiliency essential to meet the needs and expectations of your staff requires flexibility. Usually, this means letting go of the desire to control everything.

You are a leader only when people follow.

What does it take to achieve and then nurture the respect of employees? Obviously, there is no single answer, but the following suggestions will get you started in the right direction:

- Be sure you understand exactly what constitutes improvement in their area of responsibility.

- Develop a system for measuring progress objectively.
- Insist that they check their recommendations with others affected *before* you get them.
- Don't dwell on their past mistakes.
- Clarify in writing the end-results that are to be achieved. What activities will lead to accomplishing the objectives? Which ones should have priority? How can a unit's objectives dovetail with company objectives, policies, plans, and budgets?

Differences between supervisors who accomplish much and those who don't are often decided by very narrow margins. Those who win are able to point people in the right direction. In today's demanding environment this means leaders who:

- Are willing to take risks.
- Are at their best under pressure.
- Can simplify complicated issues so others understand and will follow.
- Learn to analyze alternatives systematically.
- Control emotional extremes, neither sulking in defeat nor gloating in victory.
- Qualify themselves with expertise.
- Sort divergent views and formulate action.
- Discipline themselves to anticipate critical change.
- Help others succeed.
- Balance career and home responsibilities.
- Temper personal impatience with team-building requirements.
- Think of failure as an opportunity to try something new.

Encouraging people to pull with you requires such positive action. It also requires avoidance of some very tempting behaviors:

- Don't dwell on past mistakes.

Leaders must not only be *willing* to share credit—they must do it! They must show by their actions how much they want their team members to succeed.

- Don't seek to place blame.
- Don't procrastinate.
- Don't avoid accountability.
- Don't shoot the messengers of bad news.
- Don't exploit others for personal gain.
- Don't concentrate all authority at the top.
- Don't ignore facts.
- Don't trust your instincts exclusively without counsel.
- Don't defend the status quo too long.
- Don't allow temper to cloud your judgment.
- Don't mistake status symbols, high incomes, and control over people and resources for leadership.

Most recent surveys suggest that employees whose jobs give them a sense of identity tend to work longer and harder. Establishing an environment in which this can and does happen is the key to success. More than dollars are involved. Respect and trust must be earned every day.

More Ways to Develop Trust

Trust develops in a work climate that encourages honesty, candor, and open communication, which implies a willingness to share work-related information freely. To achieve this, involve employees in problem solving and planning improvements whenever they are in a position to make a contribution. Listen to employees and try to see merit in their ideas. In addition you should

- Set clear goals and help employees understand the organizational objectives.
- Rearrange jobs to allow a greater degree of responsibility and self-direction.
- Realize that conflicts between the needs of individuals and those of the organization are inevitable but that these conflicts can and should be confronted openly—and resolved through the use of sound problem-solving strategies.
- Use mistakes as an opportunity to foster learning, not as a means of placing blame.
- Have high expectations of others while providing support and encouragement to attain their objectives.

Productivity Isn't Everything

Improving your effectiveness as a leader will automatically increase the productivity of your work group. But high productivity is not the only factor involved in successful management. Also important are:

- **Having a team concept.** You should care not only about the company's progress, but about the people working with you—and should show it.
- **Working on your weak points.** People who are honest with themselves can usually sum up their most important job needs.
- **Learning to delegate skillfully.** One of the most difficult duties is learning to let go of an old job. Being willing to delegate is not enough; the delegation must be done thoughtfully and skillfully. Over-delegation is as damaging as under delegation.
- **Being realistic about inadequate employees.** You cannot let incompetent people drag you down. Once you lose con-

fidence in a person and efforts to help that person have failed, you must have the courage to make a change.

- **Developing confidence.** Nobody is born with confidence; it must be developed. Confidence stems from successful accomplishments, and you can build on it day by day.
- **Concentrating on preparation**. Good preparation breeds confidence. Combining preparation with enthusiasm will enable you to put your ideas across successfully.
- **Being flexible in your thinking.** Don't think in black and white. Examine the other person's viewpoint carefully.
- **Looking to the future.** Do not be satisfied with past successes. Each new job has its own standards for accomplishment.
- **Using time wisely.** Concentrate on your most important responsibilities, and schedule your time accordingly.

Plan for the Development of Others

When you are a manager or leader, you are responsible for improving and creating the best climate for stimulating the development of those who report to you. This includes:

- A sound organizational structure.
- Job descriptions focused on results and performance standards.
- Short-term priorities that integrate with the organization's plan.
- Thorough screening of new employees.
- Management training for individuals and for groups, both within and outside the organization.
- A management-succession plan based on forward-looking evaluations.
- Advanced methods of performance review.
- Compensation based on performance.

TEAMWORK: CONVENIENCE OR SURVIVAL?

Here's a not-so-trivial question to ponder the next time you see geese migrating. Did you ever wonder why they fly in a "V" formation? Scientists have discovered the answer, and it has some powerful implications for both employers and employees.

As each bird flaps its wings, it creates an uplift for the bird immediately following. By flying in a "V" formation, the whole flock adds at least 71 percent greater flying range than if each bird flew on its own.

Whenever a goose falls out of formation, it suddenly feels a drag and resistance because it no longer benefits from the lifting power of the bird immediately in front. **Teamwork Lesson: Every member's effort is important.**

When the lead goose gets tired, he rotates back in the wing, and another goose flies point. **Teamwork Lesson: It pays to take turns doing hard jobs.**

The geese honk from behind to encourage those up front to keep up their speed. **Teamwork Lesson: An encouraging word goes a long way.**

Finally, when a goose gets sick, or is wounded and falls out, two geese fall out of formation and follow him down to help and protect him. They will stay with him until he is either able to fly or dies, then they launch out on their own and join another formation to catch up with the group. **Teamwork Lesson: Loyalty helps individuals and strengthens the group.** Unfortunately, many signs indicate that organizational loyalty is on the wane.

REVERSE THE DECLINE OF LOYALTY

The advantages of employee loyalty to the organization are as great today as in the past. A loyal employee will not quit under pressure, nor even upon personal and career reversals. A loyal employee is not likely to steal, to file false expense account records, or to use company equipment for personal projects. A loyal employee will respond rapidly and affirmatively whenever a customer, competitor, or anyone else badmouths the organization. Finally, a loyal employee is more likely to help owners bounce back when they experience a setback.

In spite of these advantages, organizational loyalty has been declining generally in recent years, due to changes in society and in the rise in corporate mergers, acquisitions, and downsizing. There are three things you can do to make employee loyalty more certain.

1. **Build teams in every unit.** When people feel isolated at work, they tend to withdraw and become increasingly narcissistic.
2. **Use performance goal-setting to build commitment.** The face-to-face aspect of goal-setting is highly important for today's employees.
3. **Be generous with recognition.** Praise, rewards, recognition, and belonging are the only things you can consistently afford that generate long-term loyalty.

AN EQUATION FOR SUCCESS: BE CLEAR ABOUT YOUR PERSONAL PRIORITIES

George Odiorne, a long-time friend and a top management consultant, developed this formula for success:

$$\mathbf{S} = \frac{A}{E}$$

It means that success (**S**) equals the amount of achievement *(A)* over the amount of expectation from bosses *(E)*. So if you achieve what you consider to be a lot *(A)* but those who rate your performance expect more *(E),* you will not be considered a success.

To be a success, you have to accomplish at least what is expected. But what if you can't? Maybe you have promised more than you can deliver, or perhaps others have set unrealistic goals. *The answer:* Communicate with your boss in advance so realistic goals can be set.

Likewise, if you're the boss, consider sharing the equation with your employees. Follow up by making sure they know exactly what you expect. I have observed that far too many owners, managers, and executives fail to let people know their personal priorities. Although you might call them idiosyncrasies, I strongly believe your employees need to know them, and it is far better that they find them out directly from you. If you do not do this, you decrease the chances of a successful relationship and increase the odds of failure.

For example, here are the things I tell people about me before we start working together. I think it is preferable to discuss these personal priorities in the final interviewing process:

- I work best with goal-oriented people who are committed, want to be accountable, display a sense of urgency when needed, and get on with the job at hand.
- I work best with people who treat commitments as final. If they sense a delay, they advise me immediately, not with an excuse but with a new commitment. In these circumstances, I expect them to minimize the delay.
- I work best with people who can tell me—at any time—their top priorities and action plans.
- I work best with people who inform me of their critical problems before I hear it from others. Cover-ups are inexcusable, and surprises are self-defeating.

- I work best with people who leave word of where they can be located when they are away from the office during business hours.
- I work *least* well with people who are defensive. I have little tolerance for excuses and prefer an admission of a mistake with either a corrective action plan or a request for help.
- My tolerance for mistakes is based on evidence that they will become learning experiences.
- I try not to shoot the messenger of bad news, and sometimes find I must be reminded.
- If you are facing uncertainty and think I can be helpful, talk with me. But remember, the more you need me, the less I need you!
- I do not bear grudges. I believe we can disagree without being disagreeable and without it negatively affecting our working relationship.
- One of my weaknesses is a tendency to discuss new projects, resulting in potential conflicts with existing priorities. If this happens, please do *not* assume that the new project has a higher priority without consulting me further.
- I believe that every important project or goal needs a champion. Therefore, leaders must think carefully about *what* they champion and about *when* and *how important* the final results will be to our overall success.

MOTIVATE WITH MORE THAN MONEY

One of the most paradoxical features of the Chicago Bears' 1985 championship season was that they could perform so superbly while being the lowest-paid team in the National Football League. Somehow their low pay didn't damage their performance on the field week after week. This highlights the misunderstanding that creeps into management thinking about the role that compensation—pay, bonuses, benefits, prizes, and rewards—plays in managing an organization.

Sure, people work for their own self-interest. But self-interest isn't expressed in dollar terms alone. While money is a need, it isn't the only need, and for many people it isn't even the most important need. The most effective motivators for highly competitive people are achievement and recognition.

An adequate pay system will get a fair day's work from people, but it won't excite anybody. Unfair pay knocks you out of the ball game. Fair pay keeps the clock running, but it doesn't win the game. You need something beyond money to win, and that's the vital edge that management has to generate.

If you've established a compensation system that is competitive and still want more performance, more creativity, more teamwork, and greater excellence, what else do you have to offer besides money?

- **Give people prestigious work.** Once the desire for money has been fully satiated, unfulfilled ego hunger may still exist.
- **Give people a sense of power in their jobs.** People quake when the tax man calls, thus the lowest paid IRS employee feels a thrill when some millionaire or titan of industry sits sweating before her, awaiting judgment. The pay may be rotten, but the power is heady. If you can design jobs in your organization in such a way that people can acquire and build power in the performance of their jobs, they will often accept less pay.
- **Give people a sense of achievement.** When people have the feeling that they are doing great things, they perform without an overriding concern for money. When people can't find achievement in their work, or if accomplishments are

concealed, you can bet your bottom dollar discontent over pay and benefits will arise.

- **Give recognition.** The organization in which good work is recognized in tangible ways—in addition to money—is likely to experience both a constancy of effort and a persistently high level of performance.
- **Give people a sense of belonging.** The organization that makes a point of selling its people on the prestige of being associated with it produces a very tangible result that can be measured in terms of performance and a lowering of the level of pressure employees place upon the organization for more money. People *do* work for money, but they also want participation, recognition, belonging, and achievement. When they get these other things, they aren't so likely to be obsessed with money, at least not when minimal standards of fairness are met.

Nordstrom

Retailer Nordstrom has built so strong a culture around serving the customer (weeding out any employee who doesn't buy the idea) that the entire employee manual is a five- by eight-inch card with one rule on it: "Use your good judgment in all situations."

LITTLE THINGS MEAN A LOT

The little things you say—or don't say—can make a big difference in employee morale and productivity. How many of the following "little" words and phrases are a consistent part of your oral and written communications?

- **We**—One of the quickest ways to build a sense of teamwork is by using "we" instead of "I" whenever possible.

- **Please**—Saying this regularly may not seem too important, but neglecting it quickly leaves employees feeling unvalued.
- **Thank You**—Awards and recognition programs for outstanding employees are great, but you shouldn't neglect thanking employees for their everyday contributions, too.
- **Good Job**—Let people know when they've done something right—and what that right thing was. Then watch how quickly they do it right again!
- **Keep It Up**—One reason projects fail is that people lose their enthusiasm halfway through. Consistently encouraging your team will help create the momentum they need to finish the job.
- **How Can I Help?**—Your willingness to follow your employees' lead empowers them. It lets them retain ownership of the problem while letting you know where they need assistance.
- **What Do You Think?**—Asking employees for their views shows that you recognize their expertise and value their opinions. It may also provide helpful insights from the people most likely to be affected by your decisions.
- **How Do You Feel About It?**—Although you certainly won't run your department purely on emotions, taking into account the "feeling" side of business can head off many potential problems.
- **I Was Wrong**—It's hard for any of us to admit our mistakes, especially when an employee was right and we were wrong. Willingness to do so, however, is essential to any supervisor's credibility.

These words and phrases have power out of all proportion to their length. Delivered consistently and sincerely, they can significantly improve morale and increase productivity—not a bad payoff for a "little" investment.

When criticism is necessary,

- **Express understanding** of the performance problem ("I know how difficult it is to . . .").
- **Use examples** of actual unsatisfactory behavior, but don't belabor the point.
- **Make constructive** suggestions about how to improve.
- **Get a** firm commitment to correct a problem by a specific date.
- **Mention recent** positive achievements of the individual to soften the blow of the negative message.

Challenge your team, and let them challenge you.

LEARN TO MOTIVATE, NOT DE-MOTIVATE

Your approach to motivation sets the tone for those who are responsible to you. You can motivate them or de-motivate them by what you say and do. Your performance, as well as theirs, is affected by the result.

People are turned on when you:

- Challenge them with important work.
- Provide necessary support services.
- Let them know what is expected.
- Recognize their accomplishments appropriately.
- Keep them informed of changes that may affect them.
- Go out of your way to help them.
- Communicate progress regularly.
- Face up to needed personnel changes and assignments.
- Seek their advice sincerely.
- Demonstrate confidence in them.
- Encourage ingenuity.

People are turned off when you:

- Fail to give them your full attention.
- Fail to acknowledge their personal preferences.
- Belittle their accomplishments.
- Criticize them in front of others.
- Are insensitive to time schedules.
- Waiver in making a decision.
- Do not complete your part of the work.
- Are preoccupied with your own projects.
- Show favoritism.

Keep these motivational techniques in mind, and your employees will perform better, the organization's morale will be higher, and your own record as a leader will improve.

Those who help others succeed have a common name . . . leader.

RECOGNIZE PERFORMANCE

While there is little doubt that money is a super motivator, a well-deserved pat on the back can be a morale booster and goodwill stimulator. Sincere recognition for a job well done is both a motivator and a form of payment. As a method of payment for performance, it has many no-cost advantages. To begin with, there's a greater willingness on the part of people to:

- **Invest their** free time in developing ideas that affect the firm's current success and future growth.
- **Cooperate and** see points of view other than their own.
- **Think creatively** about problems blocking progress.
- **Consider ways** that work flow can be improved, down time cut, budgets reduced, sales increased, and so forth.

- **Help evaluate** new marketing, management, or production concepts.
- **Offer advice** on how to cut through red tape.

Sincere recognition is both a motivator and a form of payment.

In other words, employees whose contributions are appropriately recognized become a reservoir of ideas for improvement rather than roadblocks to progress.

GETTING HELP FROM COWORKERS AND CUSTOMERS

Allies are important when you are working your way out of a setback. If you have treated your coworkers the right way, you may be able to count on them.

It is important to cultivate allies. Not only will they share your workload, but they can be a good source of recommendations when it's time to seek a new opportunity. Most employers can tell when an ally's recommendation is genuine.

Take care of your customers, and they, too, may be there for you when you need them. If you go out of your way to accommodate customers even when it's difficult and you'd rather not, they are more likely to support you when times get tough, you experience delays, or change products. Loyal customers whom you have treated well are not likely to abandon you immediately.

The Golden Rule is never out of fashion, especially when it comes to the way you treat customers and colleagues. There's a lot of truth to the old adage, "Be careful who you kick on the way up, you never know who you'll meet on the way down!"

Which do you prefer—a store that has you wait on yourself or one that hires people to ignore you?

Are You Really Customer Focused?

Here's how to tell. Take this little quiz. Be honest!

		Yes	No
1.	Do you plan to have more customers this year? How many? By When?	☐	☐
2.	Do you expect more business from each customer this year? How much? What type? Is it the type of business you want most?	☐	☐
3.	Do you have a way to measure customer loyalty? How do you do it? How accurate and reliable are the data?	☐	☐
4.	Do you know what your customers expect from you? Is this fact or opinion?	☐	☐
5.	Does top management believe that employees at all levels are listening to customers? If not, why not?	☐	☐
6.	Can your company respond quickly to what customers tell you? If not, why not?	☐	☐
7.	Do employees get direct information about customer complaints?	☐	☐
8.	Are the employees who produce your products or provide your service directly involved in determining how customer satisfaction is measured?	☐	☐
9.	Is your compensation plan based in part on customer satisfaction measurements?	☐	☐
10.	Do you have confidence in your ability to retain your best customers, while you find new ones?	☐	☐

If you answered "no" to any of these questions, you are not yet really customer focused. To take the next step, ask everyone else in your organization to take the quiz. Compare answers. Thoroughly discuss all areas of disagreement. If you can't agree on corrective action and begin it, don't be surprised if your customers leave you.

Step 9

Will You Use Everything You Have?

John Havlicek, a Boston Celtic for sixteen seasons, was known as "Mr. Perpetual Motion." Once Havlicek started running, he didn't stop. Packed house or empty arena, crucial game or merely finishing out the season, Havlicek gave a hundred cents on the dollar! And there was more than his 100 percent effort. Hustle itself would have cloaked him with the mantle of greatness. But to that was added production, leadership, and a performance under pressure that was always steady and often brilliant. John Havlicek was the standard by which other basketball players were measured. He was the very soul of the sports expression, "He came to play."

> **The purpose of life is to be defeated by greater and greater things.**—Rainer Maria Rilke

Change isn't easy. Overcoming setbacks may require using every talent. It will also require sacrifice. First, you may need to sacrifice a few treasured notions as you assess where you've been and what you've done. You may also need to sacrifice some comfortable habits as you determine what hasn't worked and what needs to change.

Sacrifice is closely related to change. As you complete this book, ask yourself: What am I willing to give up? What am I willing to change? How much time and energy am I willing to spend?

WIPED OUT IN DEPRESSION, BANKER LEAVES MILLIONS TO SMALL TOWN

During the Depression, Harold Englehardt went from farm to farm in Lowell, Michigan, raising money for a new bank. Over years, the bank president made deals on a handshake, dressed as Santa at Christmas and passed out Halloween candy in a top hat.

Everyone suspected Englehardt was wealthy and knew he was generous, but not this wealthy or this generous: Upon his death at age ninety-six, he left $12 million, the bulk of his estate, to make life better in his hometown of four thousand. The donation dwarfs the city's $1.9 million general fund for the current fiscal year. The gift will be used to create a fund that will distribute about $500,000 in grants each year.

"You wouldn't know he was a millionaire," said Evelyn Briggs, a former neighbor. "He lived like a common man."

Harold Englehardt bounced back from financial ruin, became a winner, and then gave everything away.

> **You can preach a better sermon with your life than with your lips.**—Goldsmith

WHAT TO DO WHEN YOUR BOSS IS AGAINST YOU

If your path to recovery is blocked by a boss who is against you,

you can begin to unblock her opposition by answering some basic questions. Ask yourself:

- Why is this happening? What are her motives? What needs does she have that I am not meeting—that I could meet? What's stopping me? See if you can write your answers to these questions. Then ask a few people you trust (preferably, who know you both) if your answers make sense.
- What changes does she seek in me? Are they justified?
- What risks would I take to make her my advocate? What are the odds of converting her to become my ally?
- Do I have someone ready to take my place?
- Am I as supportive as I should be? Am I as supportive as I can be? If not, why not? In other words, have I analyzed my own motives for dealing with this boss? Have I tried to find out how she dealt with other people who reported to her?

As you answer these questions, it is important to determine whether your boss's blocking techniques are subtle or direct. For example, does she imply bad consequences if you don't do things *her way*? Or, does she say flat out, "I can't recommend you for promotion until you . . ."?

At twenty-five, we worry about what the boss thinks of us. At forty, we don't care. At fifty, we discover they haven't thought of us at all.

The most reliable way to attack this problem is through your performance review. Here are the steps to be taken.

You must *manage your performance review*:

1. Sell yourself! You're entitled to tell your boss about what

you think you do well. Turn the talk to your talents, and let your light shine. Put in a plug for what you do well!

2. If your boss brings up your mistakes, don't defend them. If they happened, admit it. Explain why they happened and what steps you have taken so that they will not be repeated.
3. Set joint expectations. You and your boss need to set up mutually acceptable goals for your performance. The Personal Performance Contract formula from my book *Personal Performance Contracts: The Key to Job Success* is an excellent way to capture and record key results.
4. When your review comes to a close, stand head and shoulders above the crowd by thanking your boss for her time and effort.
5. Write up the results of your review, and give a copy to your boss to make sure you agree on its contents and recommendations. Detail the goals you drafted, the measurements you chose, and the time period in which the goals are to be attained. Include any other pertinent details you discussed, such as points needing improvement.
6. Be proactive. Ask your boss for another review in six months to see how you are doing on your goals. She'll probably be surprised and pleased that you want to repeat the process again so soon!

The trouble with being a boss today is you can't be sure if people are following you or gathering evidence for a lawsuit.

Performance reviews can either change or confirm opinions. Plan for your review carefully so it confirms what has actually happened and sets a course for future improvement. Think in terms of *measurable results, not activities.* Remember: the never-ending quest of all leaders at all times in all circumstances to answer the question, *How do we define performance?*

- **You must build your resume from your performance review**. You can't avoid the question, "If this boss won't testify about how good you are and what you've accomplished—who will?"
- **You must see if you can negotiate a Personal Performance Contract**—a document that classifies needs, notes the importance of each one, anticipates obstacles, defines performance targets and progress measurements, and, most importantly, sets an action plan for *who* will do *what* by *when.*

The first step in the process is to agree on the key results for your job. For example, you and your boss may decide that the three key results you are to achieve in the coming year are to:

- Respond to customer inquiries.
- Spend more time with your most profitable clients.
- Gather and learn from marketplace feedback.

Next, determine how your progress will be measured. Indicators are best expressed in terms of quality, quantity, time, and cost. Sample indicators might include:

Quantity

- Number of customers/clients served per month, quarter, etc.
- Number of items processed per week, month, etc.
- Number of cases handled.
- Number of customer complaints per year.

Quality

- Error rate/ratio (by department, project, etc.).
- Production hours lost due to injury per quarter, year, etc.
- Percentage of orders without error.
- Percentage of tests repeated.
- Percentage of work redone.

Time

- Number or percentage of deadlines missed.
- Number or percentage of requests answered within five days.
- Number of days to complete.
- Time elapsed (turnaround time).

Cost

- Percentage of variance from budget.
- Dollars as line item in budget.
- Dollars saved over previous quarter.
- Dollar cost per person contacted or per order received.

For each key result area, list:

- The need (be as detailed as you can be),
- Why it is important,
- Its relative importance (should it occupy 50 percent of your time, or only 25 percent?),
- Performance targets/results expected,
- How it will be measured (quality, quantity, time, or cost),
- Your action plan (who, what, when) for achieving the result.

Finally, draw up an action plan to designate *who* is to do *what* by *when* in order to accomplish your key result. Be sure the plan:

- Details what activity or equipment is needed to achieve the planned objectives.
- Specifies when checkpoints are to be met (dates and deadlines).
- Determines which alternative courses of action should be available.
- Names all responsible people involved.

The bottom line is this: Is your boss blocking you for *personal* or *performance* reasons?

If the reasons are personal, what are they? How legitimate are they? How correctable? How critical to your future? Try

**There's no fool like an old fool . . .
you can't beat experience.**

to determine how soon, if at all, your incompetent boss will be led to the company's chopping block. Ask yourself:

1. Will upper management eventually wake up and do something about my boss?
2. Is it possible for me to make my boss's inadequacies known?
3. What is my track record with this company?
   Would my criticism be believed?
   Can I risk being labeled a complainer by upper management?
4. Can I afford having this person as my boss?

If the reasons are performance-based, how is your performance measured? How far apart are your expectations and results? How long would it take to bridge the gap?

The real world requires that you focus on becoming allies, not friends. There is only a 20 percent chance of being friends, but an 80 percent chance of being allies. If and when you decide it's hopeless and you must move on, don't burn your bridges. Find a new job, take it, and leave on good terms.

As employees gain seniority, they tend to become quieter. They have more to keep quiet about.

CAN YOU REALISTICALLY APPRAISE YOURSELF?

Bounce Back and Win began with self-appraisal, and that's how it ends. Self-appraisal is a never-ending process. It isn't something to be done once and shelved. At every stage in your career—at every stage in your recovery from defeat—you need to carefully examine your strengths and weaknesses.

Unless you are able to assess your own progress objectively, you will always be subject to misleading yourself. To assess your progress, you must ask yourself tough questions about what has happened to you, what is happening now, and what you would like to make happen in the long run. The questions that follow will help you focus on these areas in such a way that you will be able to see your true motives, accomplishments, and needs much more clearly. Coincidentally, answering the questions will also help you prepare for a performance review.

The responses that follow have been taken from examples received from my clients.

What are my best successes/judgments?

- Managing the Kansas City Region.
- Early sales career in Chicago.
- Updating the company strategy.
- Organizing the new product planning process.
- Planning and selling the year-end project.
- Managing and closing the Sears order.

What do these have in common?

- I set goals and accomplished them on my own.
- I was encouraged by others to succeed.

What was my role in these accomplishments?

- I was the creator and leader, and I was deeply involved.

What was a key ingredient toward success?

- I was highly motivated to succeed and received strong support.

What was my key attitude?

- Confidence that I could succeed, and determination.

What are my worst defeats/judgments?

- Failure of AMP program.
- Dealing with family problems.
- Time as Director of Central District.

What do these episodes have in common?

- I was responsible for creation.
- I was in charge.
- I was not prepared.
- I lost support from others.

What was my role in bringing about the failure?

- I tried to control too much.
- I let personal relationships fog my judgment.

What was the key ingredient toward failure?

- Lost the confidence of others.
- Over-control.

What was my key attitude?

- I thought I knew better than anyone else.

> **I've always admired the intelligence of people who aren't afraid to say they agree with me.**

What contributes to my winning when I do win?

- Good perception, analysis, and planning.
- Confidence in myself without a fear of failure.
- Tenacity, perseverance, and energy to win.
- Desire to prove myself and to please others.
- Control of my strategy without fear of being second-guessed.
- Attention to detail.

What contributes to my losing when I do lose?

- Over-attention to detail.
- Frustration, depression when not in total control.

- Letting personal relationships affect my judgment.
- Sense of insecurity, rejection, worthlessness, and failure.

What is my Achilles heel?

- Getting bogged down in detail.

What are my desired skills?

- Public speaking improvement.
- Computer knowledge.
- Interpersonal "schmoozing."
- Financial report interpretation.

What are my key strengths?

- Risk taker
- Experience
- Self-motivated
- Written communication

What are my key weaknesses?

- Insecurity
- Self-image requires constant success
- Skepticism/cynicism
- Oral communication

After you have prepared your answers, discuss them with your spouse or someone else who knows you *very* well and will tell you frankly whether they agree with your answers and if not, why not. You will then have a much better sense of whether the goals you are thinking about are realistic. You will also know whether criticisms of you are justified and praises deserved.

THE POTENTIAL FOR EXCELLENCE

On April 18, 1955, the most celebrated brain of the twentieth century was removed from Albert Einstein's body. Dr. Thomas Harvey, a pathologist at Princeton, where Einstein died, announced that a team of experts would seek a clue to the mystery of Einstein's genius by examining his brain. What were their findings? As great as Einstein was, he was still more like other human beings than unlike them. The experts found his brain to be just like yours and mine. The potential for excellence can be found in each of us.

WHY LOSERS LOSE

Are losers born or made? Are Americans so focused on winning that they forget why losers lose? Since losing is much more common than winning, how can we learn more from our losses?

Here is a quick and easy way to see where you stand. Rate yourself in each category as follows:

1. Applies to me most of the time.
2. Applies to me 50 percent of the time.
3. Applies to me some of the time.
4. Rarely applies to me.
5. Never applies to me.

Then total your responses.

	Circle One
Prepare casually.	1 2 3 4 5
Tolerate excuses.	1 2 3 4 5
Don't learn from mistakes	1 2 3 4 5
Count on outside help.	1 2 3 4 5
Am easily discouraged.	1 2 3 4 5
Don't set new goals.	1 2 3 4 5
Blame others.	1 2 3 4 5
Expect easy victories.	1 2 3 4 5
Allow easy victories.	1 2 3 4 5
Repeat past errors.	1 2 3 4 5
Avoid difficult tasks.	1 2 3 4 5
Am quickly distracted from long-term goals.	1 2 3 4 5
Commend mediocrity.	1 2 3 4 5
Accept unearned rewards.	1 2 3 4 5
Am not self-disciplined.	1 2 3 4 5
Associate with losers.	1 2 3 4 5
TOTAL	________

The only security in this world is found in knowledge and persistence.

To keep our lives in balance, we must find ways to cope with losses and build on wins. Your honest rating on this quiz will help you determine where to focus your attention.

If your total score is:

0–30—You are your own worst enemy.

31–41—You have a long way to go.

42–52—You are strongly motivated to improve.

53–63—You are *poised* to be a winner

64–75—You are *favored* to be a *consistent* winner.

Never say "Poor me."

If we are blessed with normal physical and mental health, we all have options. We can make decisions. Some will be good, some bad. Thank God, when we make bad ones we have another option. We can withdraw or bounce back. May this book give you the confidence, the incentive, and the tools so you will never hesitate to *Bounce Back and Win!*

We're not in this to test the waters, we are in this to make waves.

About the Author

Roger Fritz is considered one of the country's foremost authorities on Performance Based Management and change requirements for individuals. Organizations from Fortune 500 companies to family-owned businesses have used his advice. Dr. Fritz has served over 300 clients and takes time each month for keynote, workshop and seminar presentations. His features in monthly magazines and weekly columns in business newspapers reach millions of readers. His 32 published books include several best sellers, book-of-the-month selections and award winners.

Roger passionately believes that *life is anticipation* and reveals in many captivating ways how that powerful principle changes lives and prompts success. His presentations feature unique combinations of humor, inspiration, practical advice and the impact of personal accountability.

He is founder (1972) and president of Organization Development Consultants, 1240 Iroquois Drive, Suite 406, Naperville, IL 60563 • Phone- 630-420-7673 • Fax 630-420-7835 • Email: RFritz3800@aol.com • Website: http://www.rogerfritz.com

Index

Additional Information

For more information about Dr. Roger Fritz's consulting and presentation topics or for a catalog of books, audio tapes, CD-ROMS, reprints, software and other products, contact:

Organization Development Consultants
Phone: 630.420.7673
Fax: 630.420.7835
Email: RFritz3800@aol.com
Website: http://www.rogerfritz.com